MECHANISM OF ACTION

Tales from Retail Pharmacy, Race Matters, and Resilience

A Memoir

Angie LaShaye, PharmD

ATG

ISBN: 9798993863917
LCCN: 2025924123

angielashaye.com

ATG

DEDICATION

To my parents I thank you both for every sacrifice seen and unseen, that you have made. I am eternally grateful for every prayer sent on my behalf by you, my grands, great-grands and extended loving family. To the four other people that raised me, my lack of cs was remedied by all that you older sibs taught me. You all bless me in unique ways. I cannot imagine this life without you (hug emoji). To my good friend and XUCOP buddy, thank you for your input and for tolerating your absent-minded, unaware friend for so many years. To my kids, I thank God for choosing me to be your mom. Take advantage of every opportunity God grants you. Give your best towards each endeavor and you won't have any regrets. To my Love, my PB, my Best Friend, we've spent most of our lives together at this point. We've persevered through the thin, thick and thicker. I think it's safe to say we're going to make it (smile emoji). It's me and you against the world. Know that I will always love you.... almost as much as I love Jesus (laugh emoji, hug emoji). Thank you for everything.

Contents

INTRODUCTION

This memoir was written by me, Dr. Angie LaShaye, a community pharmacist spilling tales of the untold from retail pharmacy and the college years without violating HIPAA. Hopefully my undiagnosed "executive dysfunction" doesn't cause too much disruption while recounting these stories. Some of these stories are unbelievable. Some may make you laugh; jaw drop or just make you feel sorry for me. I'm ok with that. A few of these tales are not my own but were shared with me as a matter of fact not fiction and not necessarily in chronological order. Most of the names have been changed but the situations are the same. For anyone who told me anything that I did not get quite right in intricacies due to years gone by and an imperfect memory, consider that the Holy Bible was written in a similar fashion. Matthew recounted things a little different from how Luke recounted things. The truth was still told. The outcomes remain the same.

Mechanism of Action was written for curious individuals who pick up prescriptions at the pharmacy and most definitely for those who work behind the pharmacy counter. I serve as a member of a profession that is a part of nearly everyone's lives. Whether you serve as the provider or the consumer, human encounter is a centerpiece of the overall experience.

And as long as there are human beings on either side of the counter of community pharmacy, there will be drama. It can be hard to believe. The pharmacy profession seems so boring.

Why write about it? Well, my career has been anything but. While empathy will always be prioritized for the customer because they are also patients, hopefully you'll gain an empathetic disposition after reading this short memoir for those who work in an underappreciated profession.

This memoir is especially for all my old school fellow community pharmacists who tolerated years of fast-paced chaotic work spaces without lunch breaks, endured the worst of the opioid epidemic, fake prescriptions, receiving "thank you's" one minute, then salty insults the next. For having to explain for the umpteenth time why Alprazolam cannot be filled 10 days early, and the ever-elusive work-life balance. I know you're tired. Whether you're still hanging in there full-time for the love of the profession or even the fear of lingering debt, stay calm and remember the pharmacist's prayer: "Dear Lord, please give me the strength to not jump over this counter…" You know the rest (lol emoji).

While this read is in part a *read* on certain big chain pharmacies, my pharmacy peers, unruly customers, and unavoidable race matters, I do not spare myself in the details that I do tell. I wanted to share my experiences and my perspectives. I do not seek to claim righteousness here. It would be arrogant to pretend to have all the answers to issues within a problematic profession that I willfully took part in. Whether intentional or not, it proves to be nearly unavoidable to compromise personal values to satisfy customers and the company you work for. Community (aka retail) pharmacy is almost a completely for-profit business that relies on copays, insurance, costs, technology, PBMs, government regulations, and patient outcomes. There will always be a dichotomy of what is considered to be right or wrong in this practice. No one is innocent. No one is righteous.

There are several instances where I place a magnifying glass over experiences that would be incomplete if not inauthentic without including trials that were embedded within this profession for minorities and women who dared to achieve any level of success in spaces that were dominated by white men. Not that I'm trying to ignore that white male peers in this profession also experience difficulties. None of us are exempt from the problems that occur in those work spaces. However, not everyone can claim the extra hurdles of racial discrimination and gender discrimination. I am an African American woman. My point of view as it relates to some other people and pharmacy personnel will resonate with some and register distant with others. I offer no apology as my views over what I experienced first-hand, especially in the early part of my career living in the Deep South, is the effect not the cause. But after so many years and so much diversity within the profession, I'm glad to say that attitudes towards race and gender have progressed on both sides of the counter.

So, I don't expect every pharmacist to agree with me. Not everyone has had such a dramatic experience as mine worth writing about. Many have gone unscathed, enjoying working in this business every day and have had the best careers. I haven't necessarily met those pharmacists. What we can all agree on, however, is that, much like our personal lives, this profession can be complicated and unpredictable. That stated, at the end of the day, we are like everyone else. We *all* want our presence to matter. In our personal lives we want our contributions to matter to our loved ones. In our professional lives we want our contributions to matter to those we serve, to have some job satisfaction and no regrets by the end of our careers. Plus, as you'll discover in this memoir, people do not have a clue as to what goes on in this profession and behind that pharmacy counter. There is never a dull day.

PART 1:
THE PROFITS AND PERILS OF RETAIL PHARMACY

MECHANISM OF ACTION

1

DETAILS MATTER

It started as a great day at the "Three Letter Pharmacy" in Newnan, GA. Fall was in the air. Halloween of 2017 was just around the corner. Dreaded seasonal dander that managed to filter into the pharmacy air ducts was starting to disappear. We'd set up a goodie bowl at the pharmacy check-out counter to hand out to anxious children in the spirit of the occasion. I was having the usual casual conversation with the pharmacy technician working with me before the day busied itself. A few minutes later an adorable little gap-tooth kid about 7 years old, with dimples grinning devilishly from ear-to-ear, darts to the pharmacy counter out of nowhere unaccompanied by his parents.

"Hi!" he said excitedly.

His smile and those eyes, so gray and wide, were giving away the guilt of whatever he might have done just seconds before. I greet the little blonde rascal with a, *what have you done and where are your parents,* kinda smile,

"Hey there! What are you up to, cutie?"

"Nothing." With that devious grin.

I looked around. Still no parent to claim him. I see a woman in the OTC section but she never looks his way. I then reach for the goodie bowl that he's probably after in the first place.

"What are you going to be for Halloween?" I asked.

"Yo mamma!"

Mouth wide open, now frowning, I turn around stunned to look at my tech who's already looking at me just as stunned. She then resumed her morning duties without ever saying a word.

"Boy!"

A thirty-something year old father appeared from one of the aisles finally catching up with his mischievous child.

"Where did you get that from?" He asked.

"He got it from you!" I replied on the kid's behalf.

"Nuh, unh! No, he didn't!" Shaking his head vigorously. He's now close enough that I can see the matching gray eyes.

"No. I don't say that! Say you're sorry right now!" He reached for his son's shoulder.

"Say you're sorry!"

"I'm sorry," the boy told me while still flashing that '*I ain't sorry'* grin.

I just knew the boy only complied because he saw me put the goodie bowl back on the counter. Meanwhile, the woman in the OTC section who I know by now is clearly not his mother, looked at me and simply laughed in amusement at the boy's retort and resumed with what must have been her most difficult decision of the day—whether to buy this vitamin or that vitamin. I, on the other hand, am thinking of a hundred other occupations where I would never get the response 'yo mamma' and then contemplating as to why in the world I chose this profession in the first place.

So young, so focused. So naïve when I started. I would have never thought I was entering a sector of healthcare that was filled with as much drama and disrespect as it was mitigation and cooperation. I'm sure my intentions were admirable once upon a time ago.

My first career choice as a child was to be a writer. As a teenager, I thought I would invent a cure for cancer. Then I'd travel the world as an ambitious career woman. That is until after taking an aptitude test my junior year in high school that assured me pharmacy was my destiny. So, I shifted my ambition accordingly. A love for science and math cultivated 6 years of collegiate study that granted me a "hare" status in the *Tortoise and the Hare* race to the finish line. Then voila! I'm Dr. Angie. As many young pharmacists can relate, I was so energetic. I used to possess so much joy and enthusiasm catering to the needs of those I pledged to serve in the open-door retail, brick-and-mortar pharmacy.

It's why we're all here—to serve. Specifically, pharmacists

provide a service in the healthcare sphere that cannot be administered in totality within a doctor's office, clinic, or hospital—and for a good reason. The liability would be outrageous. Plus, doctors and nurses would run amuck. So, you come see us at the pharmacy. It's unavoidable. You're not feeling well? Prescribed medication? Don't want it. But you gotta get it. It's a necessary inconvenience. You cannot avoid the pharmacy.

Allow me to provide the best service in the least amount of time, with the brightest smile, turning this unwelcomed visit into the best part of your day unexpectedly! Because to us, your neighborhood friendly pharmacists, you are priority #1 right now no matter what kind of sucky, sickly day you're having or how the rest of the world is treating you (or your pharmacist). We are here to serve you, giving you and your rotten kid (angel face emoji), our very best (cheezy face, jazz hands emoji)!

But, today? 'Yo mamma' at the start of the day? Today, that disrespectful little minion can say goodbye to the goodie bowl!

******

At the end of a year lease in Douglas Co., GA, my husband, Ron, and I decided to purchase what was supposed to be our forever home. After moving for the 10th time in 14 years it's not surprising that fatigue has set in with the relocation process. You've heard of the 7-year career itch? My husband got it every 2 and ½ years. Thankfully, it's been within one state in the Bible Belt. I'm not from Georgia, but I am certain that I can navigate the highways and byways better than most natives here considering the number of pharmacies I've had to float to-and-fro as a result of taking a backseat to my hubby's ambitions.

I've already chipped one unmanicured nail while unpacking and another is hanging on for dear life. As I examined the hanging nail that happened to be on my left ring finger, I also noticed a paper cut on the same finger that did not hurt until that very moment I discovered it. But instead of searching through another box for the first-aid kit to nurse my injury, I gazed at my wedding ring. It was one of two upgrades my husband purchased within 15 years. A 3ct. princess cut within a princess cut diamond, baguettes along the shank folding into a wide band of white gold. Of course, people thought it was platinum. And of course, I didn't bother to correct them. Why did we upgrade this symbol for the old ball and chain twice? I'll get to that later. For now, I'm in a state of peace and familiarity of unpacking. This time it's in a newly purchased three story home in an HOA neighborhood overlooking the fairway near the 17th hole with a bonus breath-taking lake view.

At the time, my husband and I scooped up this gem of a home at a bargain by practicing patience in a hot buyer's market and seeing an asset where others saw outdated walls, furnishings, and clutter. We visited the home previously but quickly turned away. The previous owners were baby boomers who purchased the house in cash and never seem to rid themselves of a single piece of furniture, picture wall frame, or award. They owned furniture pieces that I called "good wood" that I would have loved to have taken off their hands. But the house at first glance wasn't nearly as appealing.

Then after continuing an unsuccessful search with our second real estate agent, I did what I'd done before in our previous house hunter episodes—took a second look. Details matter. Just like in my profession, overlooking the details can cost you. The time we take making sure something is right is worth the time we save not having to fix anything that left the pharmacy wrong. As for the home, for some reason on the second time around it looked like our home.

Our backyard faced the largest of three lakes in the community. It contained about four kinds of fish. But the only kind I cared to remember were the catfish. The lake had catfish. I'm from the Mid-South where catfish is king. It was like hitting the jackpot.

The basement was unfinished when we moved in. That was the norm for the metro area. Buy an oversized house with a basement and never finish it. I decided we needed the space for retiring parents to enjoy from time to time and that my husband deserved a man cave. So, I finished it. It was over 1,400 additional sq. ft. of living space. Our modest 4 bedroom, 3 and a half bath home, is now about 4,000 sq. ft., 6 bedrooms, 4 and a half baths. In less than two years we transformed this place into a dream home.

I called that additional living space "the basement that *W Pharmacy* built." I was among a youthful generation of pharmacists that worked our butts off at an early age to earn an attractive paycheck. The skills that paid the bills—that is two mortgages, student loans, malpractice insurance, daycare, summer camp, car payments, hair care, food, uniforms, magazine subscriptions, entertainment, and 4 credit cards at one point during my career.

Specifically, I'm a retail pharmacist. "Community Pharmacist" is the preferred corporate label. We're never known or referred to as "Doctor" anything as the degree insists. We are known by our clients, that care to acknowledge us, by our first name. I was "Angie" in metro Atlanta and Chatham County, "Miss Angie" in Columbia and Richmond County, a "Pharmacy" to first gen Hispanic Americans. A "Druggist" to the elders. I was "Are you the pharmacist?" to anyone that approached the counseling window, "that Black girl pharmacist" to those who didn't think I was important enough to be known by name (never mind the name tag). I was "Hey" to that little needle size, racially ambiguous, newly licensed pharmacist I regretted showing up early to help in Douglas County. And I was a "Legal Drug Dealer" to the occasional asinine acquaintance back in the day. The position can range from thankful to thankless to downright insulting in a matter of seconds. One thing is for certain, there was never a dull day. Never.

2

STRUCTURE DICTATES
FUNCTION

Before I get into the untold topical tales from the apothecary, allow me to autocorrect a few misconceptions pertaining to the open-door corner pharmacy. A profession one would think was uneventful and monotonous. To which I'd say go strap yourself in a time machine and head over to Mayberry where they whistle while they work if that's the environment you visualized.

In case you're not familiar, the fictitious land of Mayberry is where on any given day, thirty prescriptions are dispensed by the pharmacist from A.M. to P.M. Affording them plenty of time to contact one of their friendliest patrons who happens to be an old pal from high school, informing them that the new prescription their doctor wanted them to have has a special ingredient that has to be ordered. So it'll be about a week before the prescription is available. Unphased, the patron actually apologizes on the doctor's behalf, having requested something so inconvenient. Then the patron and friend segues into a conversation explaining why they need the special medication that required the special ingredient in the first place.

In Mayberry, the pharmacist remembers to ask the patron when they were going to swing by to pick up their monthly meds which *are* ready, but not before a more important inquiry as to how they, their children and grandchildren were. Then jubilantly reflecting on last week's Sunday's sermon. But not before discussing perennials they purchased together at the local nursery several weeks ago that are now in bloom.

All of this jibber jabber wrapped in pixie dust is sprinkled through and through while the pharmacist serves a strawberry milkshake to a precocious grinning little lad who's kneeling in a tufted antique red vinyl stool at the counter. Meanwhile, as the child's antibiotic is being prepared at this Make-believe Mayberry pharmacy, the lad's mother waits patiently nearby reading a 1958 *McCall's* magazine article entitled *129 Ways to Get a Husband*. No rush. No worry.

Perhaps that tranquil scene *was* archetypal some time long ago. As for today, that depiction is merely a montage hanging in a fine frame above a bookshelf in an 80-year-old retiree's study. Today's tale tells of another.

Now we rush. Now we worry.

The modern unsophisticated patron of pills unknowingly practices naivete when approaching a pharmacy counter. To the patron it is a process of supply, demand, and purchase in the shortest amount of time possible. In the spirit of customer satisfaction and profit, any community retailer is happy to provide just that, satisfactorily. I don't know of a single living soul that desires to wait for any medication after having taken up 3 hours of their time getting ready for, going to sit down and wait your turn to be seen for 5 minutes by a primary care physician. All this after they've waited 45 minutes, then to be told that they've called in your prescription to the pharmacy. Just so you can get to the pharmacy, wait again. This time in a convoluted line of people who have lost patience with where to "drop off" and "pick up," only to be told by a technician failing to make eye contact,

"Your prescription isn't ready yet." Or worse,

"It's not in stock. We'll have your (urgent) medication in two business days."

"But today's Thursday," you might say.

"That's right," replies the tech.

"So, I won't get my medicine until Monday?"

"That's right. It'll be ready on Monday. After 3."

(Insert your reaction here)

Some version of that scenario has happened to everyone. And that's what retail service is—promises to deliver service at its best, but be prepared for the worst.

******

The modern-day atmosphere of retail pharmacy is not conducive to serve appropriately or even lawfully on a daily basis. It isn't possible with the modern design. There is a consultation window but no privacy. There are signs in some locations that read "wait here" that's typically about 6 ft. from the counter. But all can be heard and sometimes seen. All of this, by the way, violates HIPAA regulations.

Privacy violations cannot be avoided because there's always a question in broad view from someone about something in addition to the requirement to counsel upon the first fill of a prescription. However, counseling can and is often rejected by the patient. They may be in a hurry, already know how to take it, or have no intention of taking it as prescribed. They may be embarrassed, are habitually noncompliant or may feel hopeless about their situation. Or, it may be that someone else is picking up the medication and doesn't have a clue as to what it is, let alone care how to use it. New medication counseling is ALWAYS necessary. It should be the law without the option to decline. But counseling can be omitted by waiver of the patient or their representative. I can tell you from years of practice and proven data that the absence of patient counseling has contributed to up to 50% of patients administering prescribed medication incorrectly. The outcome of such negligence has resulted in a range of no reported side effects, to minor injuries to death.

To put the matter into perspective, a prescription drug is a synthetic chemical compound designed with purpose. When put to use it performs a mechanism of action that helps treat or heals someone with a medical condition. They are designed to make a difference. When you ingest, inject, inhale, or insert that man-made medicine, it will perform an action that alters a bodily function. Or it causes a chemical reaction with the natural chemicals in your body that alters some bodily function. It doesn't matter if you believe it's doing anything or not. It is a biochemical fact that structure dictates function in nature or by manipulation. Man-made drugs are specifically designed and manufactured to affect some part of the body on a microbial level in some way. Assuming there's no malfunction in the manufacturing and the physician prescribes the correct drug for the patient, if you take it correctly, it typically does what it's supposed to do. If you do not take it correctly, it can inhibit your improvement, cost you time, money and sometimes harmful side effects. It's always at least one of the aforementioned when noncompliant. But the waiver to counsel, imperfect organ systems and our bad habits may limit its effect. Noncompliance limits the effect. Abuse will yield undesirable effects. It just seems to be common sense that something we have to swallow, inhale, absorb, or inject into our bodies would mean a heck of a lot to us.

Notwithstanding that our lives are occupied more than enough; it can only benefit us to prioritize our health and well-being. Taking medication plays a part in the overall health and well-being of many of us. It is a necessary inconvenience. Pharmacists are aware that no one looks forward to the added stress of "take this, not that." It is a life changing routine to understand what a medication is for and to comply with prescription regimens. And even more important is it to listen to our bodies. But sometimes we reject change and sound advice. That decision may cause us to neglect our malfunctioning organs. As "busy bodies" marvelously designed to withstand so much, we often take our bodies for granted.

******

Pharmacists are taught to treat the disease. Physicians are taught to treat the patient. The middle ground between us is the structural foundation to help, hopefully heal and never to hurt. That is our Hippocratic Oath. Ultimately, healthcare is comprised of a system of checks and balances where no one practitioner rules. One without the other is useless. If a healthcare provider says otherwise, they're carelessly arrogant. It takes a village to raise one child and a healthcare team to help and heal a multitude of individuals. The healthcare profession is an incredible system to be a part of. There is no demographic that we do not impact. Since the introduction of the first *error* of mankind, we have been needed. It is a curse and a blessing.

I would argue though, that the healthcare professional that is most overlooked, disrespected, and undervalued is the retail pharmacist. Which is quite peculiar considering we are the limiting factor between a written order and an actual medication in hand to be consumed for miraculous outcomes. We're like the Wonder Woman of the healthcare field (superhero emoji). Although we're often treated like Robin (unamused emoji).

It should be made clear that no one in this profession is immune to problems and heartache. No matter what gender or race. All pharmacists have that in common. The public really has no idea as to what we go through behind that counter in many retail spaces. It is stressful and sometimes chaotic by design. As for the lesser seen categories of research, clinical, sales, manufacturing, and education, hats off to you. If you did not exist, the rest of us would not exist.

However, the most dramatic, stressful, and exhausting arena

of the profession, undisputedly belongs to the retail pharmacist. We belong to the family of corner brick-and-mortar, grocery store, chain, independent and specialty providers. We have a direct relationship with the consumer. We, therefore, have a direct relationship with stress. Even as brick-and-mortar has acquiesced to the evolution of online mail order pharmacies, there remains an indispensable gravitation towards the tangible. Whether they're giving a genuine compliment or a genuine profane-laced insult, customers still have an affinity to face-to-face management and delivery of their medications.

Retail pharmacists are typically paid the most but that can be eclipsed by research, sales or manufacturing depending on their performance. We enjoy that. Money. It matters. But the most rewarding aspect is by far is patient outcome. It is one of the greatest accomplishments in the world to improve the *health* and *wellbeing* of other human beings. Everyone deserves *quality of life*. We play an integral part in that. As difficult as this part of the profession can be, I implore my fellow comrades to practice humility and never forget what it's like to be on the other side of the counter. Our services make a difference. Consider people over KPIs. While no one's perfect, everyone can and should practice with integrity while fostering a moral environment. Last but not least, I encourage you to know your worth.

3

The Corner of Hell, Unhealthy and Unhappy

Any of my colleagues could have written a memoir, but not so many have seen so much in so many locations. I've had the unintentional luxury of having worked in at least 90 pharmacies since 1999 as a student, staff member, briefly as a manager, mostly as a career floater. I wouldn't advise it. Being a floater pharmacist can be head-spinning. It's ended up an unusual career that happens to fit my personality with all the relocating and pharmacy hopping. Consequently, I found it more comfortable to bounce around, avoid routine and to expect chaos. As abnormal as that sounds, the idea of monotony for me sounds terribly worse.

******

Unfortunately, chaos includes errors in the pharmacy. It does not happen often. But any error is one error too many when it involves dispensing medication. In Jefferson Parish, LA where I interned as a 4th year pharmacy student in 2002, mistakes may have happened a little too often. Or at least this one particular day it did. The pharmacy manager on this day was on a roll. First, he misfilled an antibiotic, then a blood pressure med, then something else I was too tired to even remember. I showed him the 1st, then the 2nd. When the 3rd was returned, I didn't even bother. I reprinted the label and got a new bottle with the correct medicine and gave it to the customer along with a sincere apology. The pharmacist was so overwhelmed. It was a ridiculous day when we probably needed three pharmacists but suffered one. He thanked me for coming in. Unfortunately, I had to confess that I had only come in to retrieve a red three-prong folder filled with notes that I'd left two days before. Feeling empathetic, I couldn't walk away without helping. But I had to get back to my first job—school.

That particular pharmacy was one of many corner brick-and-mortars near New Orleans in the early 2000s. It was also a 24-hr location. Twenty-four-hour pharmacies were more prevalent back then. These days those locations are so few and far in between. In part, because they lost money over time. Also, it just isn't safe.

The 24-hour pharmacy is necessarily placed near hospitals. Emergency visits are ever present and do not comply with the typical 9-to-5 operating hours. And no one wants to wait until after 9am to pick up a pain med or some other urgent medication they received a prescription for in the middle of the night. This 24-hour location in Jefferson Parish was near a number of medical facilities. Notably it was a few miles from Ochsner Hospital where Xavier University pharmacy interns were scheduled for clinical rotations. The closest hospital was Lakeside. I knew it well as it was the location of my first few obstetric visits. My doctor there allowed me to be one of the firsts in the nation to utilize 3D ultrasound imaging in color. It was my first true-to-life peak at my first born.

That corner store I called the *Hell Hole*, was the perfect location for the perfect chaos. It was always busy. The pharmacy would average about 900 prescriptions on a Monday and over 600 prescriptions during the week. The staff of six pharmacists along with I don't know how many interns and technicians, were overwhelmed regularly. There were issues every day. From the wrong drug being called in, to the wrong insurance being billed, to fraudulent prescriptions being written. Something always went wrong. There just never seemed to be a solution to prevent so many problems. Even the overnight pharmacists had it bad. They were paid more for working overnight but most of them earned it. They typically worked alone and were left with a big to-do list throughout the night that couldn't or wouldn't be done during the day shifts. It goes without saying that it was a risk to one's safety to work during those hours also. And the people they had to deal with? As the song goes, '*the freaks come out at night.*'

Overnight pharmacists are always the most entertaining by the way. I remember one in Georgia that would go to sleep on the back counter. Another who had hissy fits and habitually broke counting trays that we'd find in the morning. One white guy had a thing for Black women and loved to report when they were "feeling" him. I knew one overnight pharmacist in Chicago who would spend hours talking to family and friends while on the clock. And I cannot forget one homegirl who sent her daughter back to school after a few absences with a doctor's excuse that she wrote! You know, 'cause she's a doctor (rotfl emoji). Every overnight pharmacist I knew was a character. One of them at that chaotic location in Jefferson Parish would try to woo interns in effort to get them to stay longer. She would start a conversation right before it was time to clock out, compliment us or offer a treat or something to get one of us to stay. I thought it was hilarious. A couple of the younger interns or techs would fall for it. I'd take whatever she offered, compliment or candy, and tell her good night. I didn't consider my actions mean. We'd been warned about her protracted habits. She had no sense of urgency to complete a task and it cost her.

Nonetheless, there would be one incident after the other at that hell hole pharmacy where I interned. Much of it involving an unruly and unreasonable customer. We were blamed for every mistake, especially if the doctor screwed up. Then we'd go through hell and high water trying to correct the error by trying to get in contact with the elusive doctor that wrote the prescription. Doctors were even writing their own prescriptions, daring us not to fill them. Some were also blatantly writing scripts for addicts especially those who paid cash for their visits. The opioid epidemic had begun by that time but hadn't owned its title yet. One doctor in particular who practiced in another parish was running amuck operating an opioid pill mill. The staff pharmacists refused to fill any controlled substances from her as a result. Years later, in 2020, the docu-series *The Pharmacist*, aired on Netflix. A huge part was focused on that physician's felonious actions.

There was never a dull day in the Hell Hole, ever. If something or someone wasn't driving us crazy behind the pharmacy counter, they made up for it on the other side of the counter. There was just an aura of meanness from some of the people we served. They yelled and threw insults on any given day over the phone and in-person. We chalked it up to too many customers, with too many problems needing to be served by too few employees that they had way too easy access to. Not to mention lack of technology in those days made problem solving a parallel headache to everything else.

But some issues were customer-generated and just ludicrous. One lady tried to exchange a double D bra at the pharmacy during rush hour. Ok—it looked like a double D. Maybe even a size J. Then another insisted on a refund for polyester underwear that she had taken home and brought back. She wanted a refund on big girl panties that she left the store with! Forget that she passed the two front registers to get there. Who would have the nerve to bring borrowed panties all the way to the pharmacy?! Who would bring them back at all?!

There were plenty of incidences to speak of. The second worst incident I recall there was when a customer or maybe a passer-through decided to defecate on the restroom floor. Maybe the stalls were all occupied and her colon gave way to peristalsis? I don't know. What I do know is that the assistant store manager had to clean that shit up. He was so infuriated that he closed access to all the restrooms. He came to the pharmacy to inform us:

"The restrooms are closed! There's no sense in having them if people are just going to crap on the floor!"

Then he stormed off. Of course, he got into trouble for that later.

While some moments there were offensive, others were teachable. A 60-something year old female customer came to the pharmacy counter complaining about something that had something to do with her husband and his medication. Apparently, he kept giving her grief about taking it. So, she shifted that grief towards the pharmacy manager. The manager, who I'll refer to as "Cameron," was a charismatic white guy in his thirties at the time who could smooth talk a grizzly bear into licking the honey and the bees from a honeycomb. He effortlessly calmed the woman down and made sure she left satisfied. The idea was not to react to her anger but to give her what she wanted—respect.

As smooth as he was, Cameron was also what us Black females call "trifling." He'd cause problems then leave one of the staff pharmacists to deal with his mess. To top that off he wouldn't answer his phone if one of them called him about a matter that had nothing to do with them and 100% to do with him. Incidentally, Cameron also picked up some unhealthy cues from working with the sister girls for so long. He was used to smart mouth customers. But from time to time, I'd hear him speaking under his breath about them. He'd always have enough professionalism to not be heard saying things like,

"No wonder your ol' husband don't like you," when a female snapped at him and walked away.

I appreciated that Cameron would take the time to teach me a thing or two. It was probably because I was the only intern willing to entertain his contemptuous wisdom. He taught me how to avoid getting stopped in my tracks by customers when I was on the way to the restroom.

"Always take your [white] jacket off," he told me.

That turned out to be valuable advice early on in my career in retail. I literally could not make it to the toilet without being stopped by someone before taking a much-needed squatted pee. The old store designs had restrooms built on opposite ends of the store. Or essentially the toilet was wherever the pharmacy wasn't. Either way, it made it almost impossible to get there uninhibited. One time I was held up so long with a customer I walked back to the pharmacy afterwards, resuming my work totally forgetting that I needed to go pee.

Cameron also taught me how to make an ill-mannered customer look foolish without raising my voice or an eyebrow. It's best to keep your cool in nearly all circumstances. In a case where a customer has a conniption over their copay and wants to yell at him, he'd call their insurance company in the middle of their fit:

"Where's the pharmacist! Y'all charged me too much! I ain't never paid this much! All I pay is…"

Cameron in his calm routine would then offer to call the customer's insurance company. He'd do this using the telephone speaker (no longer allowed by the way) so that the customer could hear the full dialog:

"Hello, I'm Cameron. I'm a pharmacist calling on behalf of

[customer] in effort to verify a copay she believes is inaccurate."

"Sure! I can help you with that," the insurance agent would say. "Can I please have the prescription number?"

"Yes. It's [1234567]."

"Ok. I see that prescription," the agent responds. "This is a 3rd tier brand name medication with a copay of [$50]. There's a generic within the formulary that's covered at a copay of [$10]."

Cameron would then repeat the agent's words presumably to double down on embarrassing the customer:

"So, you're saying that the current brand name prescription that the patient requested has a [50] dollar copay but if we bill the generic instead it's [10]."

"That's correct," replies the agent.

"Thank you. You've been very helpful," Cameron concludes in his most professional tone.

"Is there anything else I can help you with today?" the agent says.

"No. That'll be all."

Cameron presses the 'end call' button then looks at the customer with false humility.

"Ma'am we can exchange the brand you requested to a generic for a lower copay if you like."

"Well, no. I'll take this then 'cause I don't want that *genetic*. It ain't the same."

"Is there anything else I can do for you ma'am?" Cameron asks.

"No thank you. Y'all have a nice day." She walks away.

"You too." He turns. He gloats. He wins.

I have to include the absolute worst incident during that time at that corner of *hell and unhealthy*, aka the Hell Hole, in Jefferson Parish, LA. It occurred during the day shift while most interns were not on schedule to work. A disgruntled elderly guy caused a meltdown because he wanted a drug that he could not have. Typical customer complaints there pertained to not being granted early refills on controlled substances like benzodiazepines or opioids. His case may have been the same. Anyway, this belligerent guy kept calling the pharmacy harassing the staff after he was denied an early refill. The final straw was when the pharmacist on duty at the time, about two years post grad, answered yet another call from the same man who was heard by her and some staff members proclaiming,

"No matter who you are or what you do you will always be a nigger."

I was speechless when told this by a senior tech from Houston who witnessed it all. He said the pharmacist, who was also an XU alum, made an inflamed comment after being dehumanized and then shut the pharmacy down. As fed up as she was with disparaging remarks from disrespectful customers, I imagine, she signed off the computers as well.

She closed the wide metal shutters at the in and out windows, refusing to dispense another prescription. The pharmacy didn't reopen until another pharmacist came in to relieve her, the manager, I believe. Our supervisor, a white male in his early forties, contacted her, possibly the next day in effort to get her account of what happened. The goal was to document the incident and then to suggest how she coulda, woulda, shoulda have handled the situation. I honestly believe our boss knew he was stepping on eggshells to even attempt to soothe her, let alone counsel her on such an egregious experience.

One has to wonder how it is that a disgruntled white person can resort to racism when they cannot have their way. Why is it that our presence and our success is such a threat? At what point were white people introduced to the lie that white was right and black along with everyone else has to get back? How long ago did we buy into this prepackaged counterfeit ideology? (If you're interested in the answer, read either version of the New York Times Best Seller, *Stamped*, by Ibrahim X. Kendi and Jason Reynolds).

That incident happened around 2002 at the influx of young female pharmacists, particularly minority female pharmacists. We all looked too young to be pharmacists, too female to have the final say, too weak to be in charge and too dark to be denying an older white man anything, let alone his prescriptions.

These incidences ranged from blatant, as it did that day, to nuanced. It was more than resorting to using pejoratives. That word is intentional. It rests in an undercover racist's back pocket waiting to be thrown at an opportune time to dehumanize a particular people when said racist has to yield to the authority of said people. They are also willfully blind. And deep down because of their blindness the racist cannot, will not accept change nor equality. To do so would require divine intervention.

What was perceived as passe´ attitudes of apathy towards discrimination by corporate heads went on for years even as the pool of pharmacists became more diverse in the early 2000s. There was no real action for change that I can recall at the behest of CEOs. No PSA. No commercial ads with young female pharmacists of color to persuade the public to embrace change back then. No action-plan. No oversight. I don't even recall an email of support over what happened, giving us an indication that this company was loyal to its young and bright minority recruits the way we were loyal to the company. DEI was grossly underdeveloped in corporate spaces. The response more or less resembled that of an unloved, unnurtured family member who didn't look like anyone else in the family. The matter was bounced back to the immediate supervisor; corporate simply looked the other way.

The pharmacy manager didn't get involved. He knew better. He just asked his colleague if she was ok. Our supervisor, who we appreciated, called the guy to ask which pharmacy he wanted his prescriptions transferred to, then banned him from the the property. One down. Way too many more to go.

4

Becoming a Pharmacist

I was rerouted to Georgia upon graduating from pharmacy school in 2003 due to life changing decisions that I made. Instead of being Texas bound (where fat sign-on bonuses were being offered), I landed in Metro Atlanta. I hit the ground running in search of employment as soon as I got there. I interviewed with a grocery store chain and two competing big box pharmacies. One of which had only resurfaced in that region a few years earlier due to a contractual obligation. Retailers were hiring just about everywhere. I knew I'd gain employment with at least one of the three. I just needed a sign-on bonus as a cushion for all of the final year and post-grad expenses I'd incurred. One company happily offered $3000 to relocate but wanted me to work at a location over an hour from where I would be living. The interview was dull and I imagined the drive to that area everyday would get tired fast. Plus, the drugs were organized according to their generic names even if they were only available in brand. I thought that was stupid.

The grocery store chain interview was totally forgettable except for my huge belly in a denim maternity dress. It had a cute little tie in the back that allowed 3 trimesters of adjustments. I had gone to the interview before a NAPLEX prep course where a group of externs including a handful of my classmates were in attendance. The NAPLEX is the licensing exam pharmacy grads have to pass in order to become registered pharmacists. My classmates and I sat together. The prep course was taught by Flipp Warrant (real name not used here), a former UGA instructor. It was excellent. They also gave sample on-campus prep courses at various universities during that time including Xavier University. We sure did appreciate that. Everyone liked Flipp. Well, everyone except one pharmacy graduate apparently. None of that had anything to do with that grocery chain interview. I only remember turning the position down. The third interview, with W Pharmacy, was the most memorable. I met the district supervisor, who I'd learned was from New York, at a location where I'd end up gaining employment.

I wore my glasses to the interview. I've needed corrective lenses since junior high school. They suit me well, ever the nerd. I only wore contacts on occasion. I prefer frames. It's just easier to put on and take them off. My 1B naturally colored hair was styled the way I'd worn it through most of my academic career, permed and in a respectable shoulder length bob with a part slightly to the left. I wore three shades of brown, earthtones, for some reason. A sleeveless turtleneck not maternity but long enough to cover my belly under a knee-length cardigan, elastic waist slacks and two-inch heal loafers that I used to think were so cute on me in college. Those heals proved to be a lapse in judgement during pregnancy as I lost my balance and nearly fell at least twice. Once while following my soon-to-be boss to the interview room. Then again on my way up two flights of stairs back to my apartment on another day.

I found the supervisor, Jared, to be easy to talk to. He was ten years my senior, tall and dirty blonde with glasses. His demeanor was professional but unintimidating. I looked him in the eye with no problem and whipped my left dimple smile at him with ease. He seemed sincere as he got to know me a little more. He asked about my work experience. I elaborated on my previous experience as an intern with the same company in Tennessee and Louisiana. What I didn't tell him was that I, like many other interns, were not cross trained and did zero tech work. Neither were we required to follow strict company policies that were always being updated. Interns from my experience were treated like we were needed instead of being taught everything we needed to know. That weakness would be exposed later at that location in Gwinnett County by the pharmacy manager. Jared informed me that this particular location was low-volume, meaning that they didn't fill many prescriptions.

"How many prescriptions does this location average?" I asked.

"About 79 scripts a day," he said.

"Oh!" I responded with a pleasant surprise. It was a far cry from what I was used to.

"My pharmacy averages 900 on Mondays and between 6 and

700 during the week." I informed him.

"Wow." He said boyishly, slightly leaning into the table between us. "You won't do nearly that many here."

What a relief, I thought. *There's no way this place could be like the hell hole I came from.*

Mid-way during the interview it occurred to me that Jared hadn't asked for my resumé. So, I cracked opened my brown leather portfolio and revealed what I thought was an above average boast of what I had to offer this company printed on thick coated, tinted Xerox paper. I proudly handed it to him. He took it. Then looked at it.

"Oh, you have a resumé?"

That is what he said when he looked at it. No joke. In the interrogative. As if all those words on stapled pieces of overpriced paper were optional.

"Yes," I chuckled in reply with an understandable expression of surprise mixed with confusion.

That was a first.

He appeared to review my resumé. A resumé that I made sure not to insert the overused term *diligent* to describe my work ethic. Then he ended the interview with a job offer followed by a "When can you start?" And something about scheduling my NAPLEX exam. That along with a wet lab and the law exam are the last hurdles to becoming a licensed pharmacist in the respective state. We walked out of the interview room. He in front of me holding the door so I could exit. I left from there totally enthused about what was in from of me in a new state with a new clientele as a new pharmacist being a brand-new mom and wife. It can only be uphill from here.

As I trailed Jared out onto the store area getting ready to leave, I remembered that I neglected to ask about a sign-on bonus. He was headed left towards the pharmacy. I was headed right towards the store exit.

"Is there a sign-on or relocation?" I asked almost walking back in his direction.

"Oh no," he responded shaking his head as he looked back at me. "We don't offer that."

His tone was noticeably different. Not mean but in a matter-of-fact or 'you-gotta-be-kidddng-me' kinda way. Then he swiftly proceeded to the pharmacy door.

5

Retail Reality Check

From that inflection point of where my career was supposed to begin after graduation, I embarked on what I believed would be a life of fulfillment within my profession. But reality had other plans. I spent 13 more years working for a pharmacy corporation that made it easy to not want to stick to one location long-term. So I chose to float early in my career after serving briefly as a staff pharmacist in a couple of locations. Not even the best customers were enough to tie me down. And I've definitely had some wonderful customers. I've also had plenty of, let's just say, inappropriate customers. For instance, there were those mature men (by that I mean old men) who could not help themselves. They had to flirt:

"You got a man?" Or,

"Can you be my girlfriend?" Then,

"How 'bout I take you home?" And,

"How much do you make? I can take care of ya." Then that one time,

"Turn around so I can see you. Your complexion doesn't need any make up."

My responses:

"I'm wearing a wedding ring. So, I guess so."

"I'll have to ask my husband."

"No."

"I'm sure you can."

(Turn around with a fake smile) "Thank you. How can I help you, sir?"

For anyone who thinks this is a perk that comes with the territory, that these are compliments that I should've considered harmless—they aren't. And I don't.

Other "perks" that come with being a floater are hearing horror stories from other pharmacists about incidences that occurred, some of which may have been why I was called to cover a shift. I frequented one location in metro Atlanta where a pharmacist was caught trying to walk out of the store with a huge bottle of Alprazolam not long before I was hired. That pharmacist was stopped by a nosey manager who asked them to open the brown bag they had when trying to walk through the exit after closing. The store managers had the privilege to stop someone including employees if they suspect theft. You should've seen the gloat on that manager's face when he told me all about it. It gave him way too much joy to embarrass people. Flexing his on-site authority which included validating his suspicions to the detriment of others was an on-the-job hobby of his. But in this case, he might have actually saved that pharmacist's life. That pharmacist had apparently become suicidal after losing their spouse and child a short time before that incident.

I'd cover PTO shifts, or when there were abrupt resignations or firings. I also covered other pharmacists during the baby boom of the early 2000s that I was a contributor of. There were multiple times I was called in to cover for a pharmacist who would go into these crying spells during her shift. She lost her mother recently and was not taking it well at all. I didn't believe the extent of her outbursts until I saw it myself. She asked me while I was working with her if I could cover her again and fill in for her next shift. I told her yes. But a few minutes later I realized I couldn't, so I had to tell her right then. The woman burst into tears right in front of me. I was so taken aback. She retreated to the rear of the pharmacy as to not be seen. I didn't know what to say. So, I said nothing and went back to work.

I met one pharmacist during an overlap shift who used to work for another company. She told me about a guy who came in as an overlap in the afternoon a few hours before her shift ended. He wore a white staff coat and company name tag. She presumed he was a floater pharmacist. But didn't verify. He came in smiling. He was slick, speaking quickly and moving swiftly. Long story short, the imposter found shelves of narcotics that were in plain sight back then and slid large bottles of hydrocodone and tramadol through the drive-thru window to someone who was waiting in a car there to scoop them up. No sooner than the staff pharmacist saw what was happening, the perp darted out of the pharmacy faster than the real pharmacist could dial 911.

Another incident I was told by a staff pharmacist involved someone posing as a maintenance worker who came in during a morning shift, using a ladder maneuvering up and down the aisles pretending to check the wiring or fixtures in the ceiling or something. The pharmacist finally scoped his movements and saw the bulk under his utility jacket. He was stuffing narcs in it. She actually tried to stop him by shaking the drugs out of his pockets.

"What are you doing?!" She yelled, in her Nigerian accent.

The guy ran out. The company fired her afterwards.

There was a break-in or rather a bust-in through the wall twice at a pharmacy I frequented in Gwinnett Co., GA. They stole narcotics, benzodiazepines, and some other easily accessible drugs. How co-inky-dinky that there was no camera footage on either occasion. No one was caught. No one was fired.

My floatation landed me in Douglas County, GA quite a bit bouncing back and forth between four locations. I didn't necessarily like either one except a location on Chapel Hill Rd. It was just a better area with a better clientele and better staff. I even met a rapper's father there. I was cool with the pharmacy manager at that location. She reminded me of my oldest sister. But she had this senior technician who was not the brightest cookie in the cookie jar. Somehow, that tech landed a district level position while remaining on site where she resolved lingering prior authorizations and unpaid claims. It was an important gig that could potentially recoup thousands of dollars. She was quirky and good for conversation but could not be left to her own devices.

During a day shift a young guy who looked like he wasn't from around these parts came in to purchase a box of diabetes test strips. I was at a nearby computer then walked over, said "hello" and initiated the transaction. The tech and I both exchanged pleasantries with the young man. He was somewhat short and attractive. He was wearing all black with a long-sleeve sweater oddly enough for that time of the year. The young man asked for a 100-count box of test strips then gave me his credit card and struck up a conversation with the tech. Meanwhile, I swiped. The card declined. I swiped again. It declined again. He then said,

"Yeah, that happens. Try doing it manually. The strip is desensitized."

He continued to talk to my tech. I'm focused on his malfunctioning card. I entered the numbers manually. It declined. I give the guy a quick side eye then walked over to the phone to call the manager to the pharmacy when the tech said,

"Wait there's a trick I can try."

She must have left her brain at home that day. Because this trick was to take the credit card and place it in one of the store plastic bags, then slide that card through the card reader.

You have got to be freaking kidding me, I was thinking while staring at her.

The card is fake dumb-dumb, another thought before rolling my eyes. Before this girl becomes an accomplice to a fraudulent purchase, I tell her to stop. I then pick up the phone and press the intercom button,

"I need a manager to the pharmacy please."

The young man knew then he wasn't getting the test strips. He was such a cute crook.

Having a rush morning in one of those four Douglas Co. locations, I see in my periphery while folding labels a woman leaning half of her body into the pharmacy consult window. At the same time, I hear beating on the counter. I turn in haste with an undeniable frown to inform the uncultured middle-aged female, void of Southern hospitality, that,

"No ma'am. we don't do that. Is there something I can help you with?"

She wanted to know if we had an OTC in stock. *So, she's not deaf and she can speak,* I'm thinking. I told her we did and where to find it. That type of service was deemed to be insufficient it turns out. In response to customer surveys, a year or so later the company ran a tv ad where this pharmacist was hurdle jumping over chairs and leaping across the aisles to get to a customer. It was intended to bolster priority for the non-prescription shopper. No matter what your pharmacist is doing, you can count on them to act like Donkey Kong chasing a banana to get to you just in time to choose the right laxative. That pharmacist looked like a clown dressed in a white jacket, tie and slacks. We were the butt of jokes. A pharmacist friend I'll refer to as, "Annette," who I shared an apartment with in college, called me specifically to taunt and laugh in my face. It was the most embarrassing commercial I had ever seen.

Why W Pharmacy? Just why?

Speaking of jokes, that same friend worked for "Wrong-Aid" Pharmacy. The name is a pun of course. But since nearly half of that pharmacy chain was swallowed by a bigger competitor that I happened to work for at the time, something had to have gone really wrong. Anyway, Annette told me about this jovial store manager she used to talk to before or after her shift. He used to share his grandiose ambitions of running his own company in Florida. He was a very nice guy by all accounts from her point of view. I thought she was very nice for entertaining his nonsense pipe dreams. The only plan he seemed to have, was telling her all about it. One morning she came in to open the pharmacy and walked in the manager's office to pick up the first till. An assistant manager who was there helping her with the till informed her that thousands of dollars came up missing and so did that jovial store manager.

"He worked the weekend and told the front-end staff to take those days off," Annette told me. We laughed and laughed! I guess Mr. Pipe Dreams had a plan after all.

******

Word on the street: I cannot prove it, but I was told that a pharmacist working west of Atlanta was kidnapped and placed in the trunk of a car after the pharmacy was robbed. He lived. But the company supposedly buried the incident. I believe it. I just can't prove it.

I *can* prove that a Three Letter Pharmacy technician was working as a pharmacist in metro Atlanta around 2006. Go on and google it. He used a legitimate pharmacist's licensing info. The imposter was hired subsequent to the district having a high turnover of pharmacists at the time. They were so desperate to cover shifts that the hiring supervisor didn't bother to run a background check or vet the guy's credentials. They didn't even verify his ID before he stepped into the pharmacy. Needless to say, hiring practices have since changed.

******

Pharmacists have been referred to as the most trusted healthcare professionals. Despite all of the stories mentioned here, it's well deserved. Just don't call us perfect. Mistakes happen although rare. With all the distractions and stress, only God knows why we don't screw up a lot more. I remember a phenobarbital dosing error that became deadly for a pediatric patient in another state. It made national news. That one shook me. As a floater it made me paranoid because customer volume and our support staff behind the counter was volatile from one location to the next. An increase in one and decrease in the other respectively were telltale signals that determined if I was filling in to work after a good day or a bad day of dispensing. Both of which can indirectly lead to a misfilled prescription. In either case, if a medication is returned to the pharmacy, the day before was definitely a bad day.

During one of my shifts in metro Atlanta a prescription was

returned that was supposed to be for pain. Instead, it was filled for a sleeping pill. The patient only noticed there was a problem because the drug she was taking was being consumed three times a day and making her extremely lethargic to where she couldn't keep her eyes open. The pain pill can cause drowsiness but not typically to point of rendering one unconscious. Albeit, it can vary person to person.

Descriptions for any dispensed medication are printed on the prescription bottles usually in the lower left corner of the label. I don't think the patient knew that but she definitely knew it wasn't the right drug. She brought the remaining tablets back. Unfortunately, it was returned during my shift. Upon looking at the name of the medication I knew exactly where to find it. We dispensed the popular pain pill every day. Similarly, when I opened the bottle she returned, I knew immediately the pills inside were the popular sleeping med. What I did not realize previously, was that the white bottles for those two medications were right beside each other on the same shelf in alphabetical order. They had the same manufacturer, same size bottle, same color and markings, different shapes. It was ridiculously easy to mistake one for the other. The only difference was that one pill was round and the other was oval. On an extremely busy day, any tech could've reached for the incorrect bottle. Well, that day happened. I had to report the incident to the pharmacy manager documenting the details the patient gave me. After pinpointing how the error may have occurred, the mix up led to corrective action and a small settlement. The pharmacist responsible was torn over the matter. It was an easy error to make if they were overwhelmed that day. I can't remember if the company implemented label and bottle scanning during that time. Those pivotal steps can be skipped by the technician who may have been rushing because a patient had arrived before their medication was ready. Per experience, the tech wouldn't have wanted them to wait for fear of customer complaints. In which case, the scanning, if it existed, could also be overridden by the pharmacist at verification assuming the same appeasement. That may have been the case here where rushing to satisfy customers was prioritized over safety.

******

A pharmacy manager I worked opposite of in a different location in metro Atlanta dispensed an antiseptic mouthwash instead of a liquid antihistamine for a pediatric patient. The kid swallowed mouthwash for 3 days. The tech that typed the prescription had a tendency to be careless. And the pharmacy manager had a tendency to disappear outside for a smoke. It was a bad habit but a coping mechanism for the constant stress there. I don't recall any adverse effects being reported; probably just fresh breath. Scribbled handwriting by the doctor aside, some regimens just don't make sense. This should've been one of them.

******

I picked up a few dreaded shifts at a nightmare of a location with W Pharmacy south of Atlanta near the airport. Anyone working for the company in or near Atlanta at that time was fully versed on the misery of working there. It's always open, always super busy, always a long line, never enough staff, always a complaint, always a high turnover. They NEVER retained staff or a pharmacy manager. I was leaving after a horrible evening shift and was so relieved that the overnight pharmacist came in on time. In a rush to high-tail it out of there, I forgot to purchase my prescription that I had transferred there.

"Crap!"

I smacked my hand against my forehead in disbelief. Knowing I was out of the medication I did a U turn and stepped to the end of the never-ending double line. The overnight pharmacist who came in unbothered, dark brown and beautiful with a mini afro seemed to be ignoring the line as if it was a requirement. Her one and only tech was stuck helping a customer at the drive-thru. It was painful to be there witnessing people clearly getting impatient and making derogatory comments aimed at the staff. There were only 2 people serving about 20 customers including me. The overnighter glanced up and saw me in one of the long double lines.

"Oh, I didn't see you there, Angie."

"I'm sorry. I left my prescription," I said with an apologetic grin, tilting my head and acknowledging my absent-mindedness.

"What's your last name?" She walked over to the bin of bagged prescriptions.

I walked to the counter scared to make eye contact with any of the angry customers. I told her my last name. She pulled the bag. Verified my info. Then completed the transaction.

"You have a good night," she said. Then she walked back over to her verification terminal as if there was no one else to tend to.

"Thank you."

I got out of there as fast as I could.

******

One might surmise at this point that I pretend to be Ms. "Do No Harm" but it's not the case. Over 20 plus years I've certainly had my share of errors. I accidentally threw away a $1200 medication in the early part of my career. It was recovered after I asked management to check the surveillance to find out what the heck I did with it. It was buried in a huge amount of plastic in the trash and was practically weightless. I was working alone that day. I realized it was missing while checking in an order that was delivered that morning by our supplier.

Some of my notable misfills occurred when dispensing hydrocodone/apap (Lortab) instead of oxycodone/apap (Percocet), Promethazine instead of Promethazine DM, and Yasmine instead of Yaz. The greatest blunder of misfills was when I dispensed a drug for narcolepsy instead of a drug for hormone replacement. That one is most memorable and disappointing because not only do the two drugs look nothing alike, but the wrong drug was sold to the patient pursuant to the prescriber's instructions to use it in an unusual way. Did the patient use the medication? Of course they did! They followed instructions.

Still to this day I have no idea how I was so distracted that something so avoidable could happen. I think we had label and bottle scanning by then. It doesn't matter if a technician typed the wrong drug in the computer or if they placed the wrong drug in the prescription bottle. It doesn't matter that I was forced to walk away from the verification terminal five times before completing that one prescription. The last line of quality control and accuracy is me. It was my fault. Distractions are ever present in the pharmacy. It has probably been the chief complaint by pharmacy staff in the retail chain for decades. But we sign on knowing the possibilities albeit some more than others.

With consideration to the busiest retailers, particularly with the one I worked for the longest, it can get overwhelming to a point that it is unbearable for any human being. Try splitting one person into three and you'll begin to get the idea. To make matters worse back then when a district or corporate representative drops in to view the disastrous show of operations that no woman or man can repair, they'd often respond in an accusatory fashion as if we want the chaos. My fellow old school pharmacists can attest to this. So, it should come as no surprise that on rare occasions in a moment of deep frustration, the pharmacist on duty at the time of the district drop-in, loses their cool and yells at the district rep and/or quits on the spot. As for myself, I've never yelled at any supervisor. Or at least I don't remember doing so (thinking emoji). I have yelled at a store manager or two, and customers, and technicians, and other pharmacists (confident emoji).

Still, it remains that distractions and moments of frustration are a part of the game. I cannot stress that enough.

As I am writing this, an article was published by NBC news pertaining to overworked pharmacists and the dangers of distractions. I can attest to being stressed and unnecessarily overworked. All the extra-curricular activities (detailing, promotions, projects, health screenings, etc.) in tandem with primary duties in the pharmacy (dispensing, customer care, consult, MTMs, insurance issues, PAs, KPIs, retention, marketing, immunizations, etc.), are a part of the reason I'd had enough of the full-time madness of retail. Although I definitely see and appreciate the role pharmacists play in vaccinating the public in between doing all the essential aforementioned.

To my knowledge, there was no such thing as pharmacy health screenings, MTMs, detailing, retention action plans or even onsite immunizations for that matter over two decades ago in the retail setting. Add those responsibilities to the ever-existing daily routine of being pulled in all directions all the time for 8 to 14 hours straight without a scheduled break and you just might lose your mind. But for God's grace (and probably medication) did we maintain our sanity.

But if you happen to visit a job board these days for a retail (community) staff pharmacist or managerial position, read the description. You'll quickly determine that we were indeed crazy enough to apply for and accept daily chaos. Hopefully we all did it because we all care about those we serve. Undoubtedly, we all did it for the money. However, if you accept mediocre pay for primo responsibility that's your fault. Know your worth. Know the responsibilities for the position you apply for and negotiate accordingly. Mediocre responsibilities warrant mediocre pay. Primo responsibilities require primo pay. So if you don't like what you do, make an exit plan. If you don't like what you're paid then negotiate or move on. Alternatively, you can post on a work-n-gripe blog or get a good laugh from comical pharmacy reels like many of us do on social media.

For my peeps who are unaware of the profits and perils of retail pharmacy, do your research before signing on the dotted line. The variables in the pharmacy can be many. We juggle way too much at one time. Yet, the errors are very few. At least they should be. The bottom line is, we get paid to NOT mess up. People get upset if we do and rightfully so.

******

As the saying goes, *you catch more flies with honey.* Too often as a floater I run into an arrogant individual. Or someone full of pride. They wear an invisible sign that reads '*I know everything there is to know. You on the other hand don't know shit.*' All of which implies for me, the stupid visitor, to just do what they say when they say and that day will be a good day. It's the typical attitude of staff members who dread when a guest (the stupid floater pharmacist) has to cover a shift for another staff member. The best response is to go with the flow. Don't be brand new. They hate that. You will be negatively critiqued for doing so. Technically, this can be said for any newcomer at Any Job, USA. In the case of the floater pharmacist, though, staff will beg their supervisor to not allow those disruptive floaters to return.

******

My usual MO is to speak first when walking through the door. Wash my hands; especially in the middle part of my career I did it a lot. When you're on a diuretic, especially Chlorthalidone, it is a given that you will wash your hands. Because you WILL PEE OFTEN. Then I disinfect counters if it's an opening shift—a habit I adopted long before the Covid pandemic thanks to a fungus I caught and some unsanitary experiences. I assess the staff if there are any. Assess the environment and raise shutters if it's an opening shift. Log in to the computer. See what "to-do" notes await at my terminal for the day. Determine if all "to-do's" will get "to-done." Check the work queue, check the printer, check the fax, check the drive-thru. Check the fridge. Check the register because the last thing you want to happen when an old school customer pays with cash is the surprise of a bare register with no till because management forgot to put it back in after opening the store. Check for Sudafed. Remove the Sudafed. Place my Red Bull and Smart Water by my terminal. Then get ready to rock and roll.

I make small talk or long-winded talk depending on how much I have in common with any staff member:

"You're a mom? I'm a mom!"

"You're a wife? I'm a wife!"

"You got a side gig? I dig side gigs!"

"You invest? To invest is the best!"

"You watch *This Is Us* and *Insecure*? Me too! Let's talk!"

******

I don't claim to be special, depending on your definition of *special* (goofball emoji). As I've mentioned, any retail pharmacist could've written a book centered around work experiences. There's plenty to tell. Many would probably make it short because we, by nature have short attention spans and require that all topics be kept to a minimum, getting to the point. As a result, I've started and stopped this long short story at least 20 times. My ability to focus is either fried by stress or never existed consistently. This profession fosters mental fatigue that can only be remedied by medication or retirement. I've noticed that I don't think as quickly as I used to. And I don't bet against the possibility of "drain bammage." Still, by nature, retail pharmacists are multitaskers which spill over into our personal lives. It's a great habit for work, not so much at home.

Imagine being *here*, but you're thinking about something over *there*. Then you get up to go *there*, but *this* has to be done before you get *there*. You complete *this*, then go *there*, but remembered you never finished what you were doing over *here*. So, after being *there*, you hop right back over *here*—right back where you started. Hopefully, you won't be disturbed before you're done with whatever you didn't finish over *here*. Now you may be thinking, '*I do that all the time.*' But you never do it while dispensing people's medications. That, my friends, is a moment in the life of a retail pharmacist.

The average retail location, which would demand swing shifts and being pulled in every direction possible, with the intent to never make a mistake, is mentally and physically draining. Even for a young graduate hungry and enthusiastic from broke-ness, it gets exhausting fast. It's the way of the beast of big pharma. They demand the most with the least. It saves them money, costs you good customer service, and costs us our sanity. Then the big wigs of big pharma earn big bonuses for it all.

I remember being so exhausted early in my career not even 30 years old. There were no lunch breaks. We would eat when or if we had overlap. Otherwise, we just had some dissatisfied customers who were forced to wait few minutes for us to scoff down our food and get back to work. We stood the entire shift most days. A lot of pharmacists purchased TED hosiery for the varicose veins that started to appear. We were never not interrupted. The phones ring off the hook:

"Pick it up by the 3rd ring, Angie," one manager would say.

You pick it up by the 3rd ring, I'd be thinking.

I can only do three things at once. Then another phone rings, and another. Then someone steps up to the consult window and the drop-off window and the drive-thru at the same time. Everybody wants your immediate attention. But there's four prescriptions 5 minutes overdue that's ruining your 'ready by promised time' stats. You tell me who or what's most important in this realistic scenario.

There's a technician working who, like the pharmacist, does not have the ability to clone herself. We're not happy with the customer service and of course the anxious customers are not happy with our customer service. Who then, is happy? The corporate executive on the golf course responsible for cutting work hours at our expense is happy. Because it's Saturday and no one can or will contact him about the misery he's inflicting on his store level employees and the people we serve. Just the other day one of my brothers was sharing his frustration of the long lines he endures when picking up his meds, having his toddler son with him, and after having worked all day. No one looks forward to that. Customers don't deserve that. But it is a part of the mess corporate execs have made. How ironic is it that during the pandemic, in the fourth quarter of 2021 as store employees have had enough, corporations cannot pay enough to keep store level employees amid the dysfunction they helped to create. Yet the current chaotic model filled with long lines, unhappy customers and overwhelmed staff, is profitable believe it or not. Therefore, corporate execs bare no consequence in the matter. I would have to thank companies like Amazon for gaining some skin in the game and inadvertently helping the retail environment improve to some degree. They get it. Mail-order is a blessing. You cannot have customers constantly in your face and do your job satisfactorily.

******

Early in my career around 2005 while working in Gwinnett County, GA, I became a staff member at a 24-hour pharmacy. It was the busiest location in that area at the time. It felt like I was working nonstop. Before I knew it, I was so fatigued over a period of time that sleep became an elusive luxury. I was blindly choosing work over health. It's comical yet pitiful to hear the phone ring at home and I'd answer,

"Thank you for calling W Pharmacy. This is Angie…."

The phone ringing at work. All my brain could think of was,

"Our Father Who art in Heaven…."

No joke! I did that once. During one shift there, I was standing at the verification computer in the middle of reading a prescription image on the screen. The next thing I knew, I was regaining consciousness.

I fell asleep with my eyes open! I thought to myself.

Months later I told my mom what happened. She replied to me with a concerned tone,

"You probably had a seizure."

That never crossed my mind.

Early burnout in this business is common. But I believe, like other young pharmacists may have, that I considered everything I was consumed with to be normal at the time. Fresh out of college embarking on real-life at full speed, 100 miles an hour. Particularly those of us who signed on for careers in addition to ready-made family life. We have this full-time job that was impactful yet stressful that did not allow the pharmacist a real break. We worked swing shifts that led to lack of adequate sleep for fear of oversleeping. The work days were nonstop. We give our digestive systems a workout by swallowing half eaten food while on the clock. If we paused and sat to eat properly like a human being the work just piled up in the meantime. Mind you, pharmacies did not close for lunch back then as they do now. So, if a customer shows up and their prescription is not ready, you better believe we got up and choked to swallow whatever's in our mouths to get it ready.

I have to give it to the Millennials. They said "no" to that bullshit work life. They really have the nerve to up-and-leave a job with zero prospects in front of them when they were fed up with retail. It was a first. Gen X did not have the brass. Even debt didn't scare the generation after us. My generation? The most we'd dare to do is call-out, go on extended vacations or have a go-to floater (like myself) who would make themselves available when a staff member became "sick" and needed coverage. In hindsight, the Millennials did what we should've done. Showed some courage. Said *'screw this'* to corporations that took us for granted and walked away.

As for myself, a member of the used and abused Generation X, I fell in line with the status-quo. *Fear.* We worked too hard and sacrificed too much. I don't really remember enjoying much of my 20s because my head was to the pavement. Just like my husband. We were busy building something. We were raised to persevere and to stick with it. We were also raised to be responsible for something and someone other than ourselves. We dove head-first into that ready-made package of career and family. For me, that included personal responsibilities of being a mother to a rambunctious toddler who I held with my left hand and a precocious baby whom I held in my right arm by then. Plus, a spouse, a full-time job, and a home to take care of. Exercise was somewhere in the picture. I developed a short fuse at some point that I partially managed by maintaining a life of prayer, church and faith. That is, until I found myself having had four jobs in one year. Then I gave in to an antidepressant.

For a long time, I was foolishly attempting to fulfill the impossible all while trying not to neglect close family members who lived 6 to 12 hours away from me and friends who were just as far away. All that I (and my peers) considered to be a life of normalcy, was actually abnormal and eventually took a toll. Idealistically, it works because it has to. It's the journey we chose. Realistically, though, at some point, something has to give. Sooner or later, you crash and check out mentally and/or physically.

The question is why so much so soon in the first place? Career, money, marriage and kids, and not necessarily in that order in my case. Just ask someone who did all of the aforementioned immediately after finishing their schooling whether high school or college. The answers may not vary much at all. My peers were ready to get on with their adult lives. Some grew up poor and desperately wanted a better way of life; to afford better opportunities for themselves and their offspring. They envisioned a career as a pharmacist to be two-fold, being of service to others while offering a better financial platform to build a family upon. A few were born in to it having parents or grands that owned pharmacies or were employees in and around the profession as teenagers.

Some classmates already had families while in pharmacy school. How they managed to do so, to me, is unbelievable. Some had overbearing parents that pressured them into a high-paying career, prestige, and family simultaneously. I knew this specifically to be the case with 1st gen American classmates growing up with immigrant parents. I was even told of how some parents compared my fellow pharmacy peers to their other relatives, taunting them as to how much money their cousins or other friends' children were making, how lavishly they lived and how big their houses were and how much they cost. Like it's some sort of race or the pursuit of happiness. My reason for taking on career and family so young and so fast was much more simplistic. Like I mentioned, I did it all, just not in order.

As it turned out, many of my peers used the profession to eventually serve as a gateway. Having some financial security, they segued into various side gigs. I heard of pharmacists embarking on multiple side hustles from becoming real estate agents, self-professed successful entrepreneurs, public speakers, self-help gurus, manufacturing and marketing their own skin care line and even becoming professional comedians. The spectrum of deviation from the profession is humongous. Although I had at least one classmate who decided to become a *real doctor* and went on to medical school. I don't recall another profession back then where so many ventured out after investing so much time and money into becoming one thing just to ultimately want to do something else.

6

Cold Compress

As a working woman I am fully aware of the disparities we all face in the professional world especially when we do not have a seat at the table. In many professional environments we can be at the table and still be ignored as if we were a part of the décor. With that in mind, I do not believe I exaggerate when I say that Black women are the most disrespected human beings on Earth. If I lie then call me a liar. But then I'll have to show you the receipts.

I believe that love conquers all and kindness wins. But in this life a sister can be pushed to kick kindness to the curb. It is an overwhelming burden to ignore belittling comments from customers. Especially when it appears to be gender specific, whether nuanced for blatant, making it that much more difficult to hold back emotions.

It was difficult for a young Black female pharmacist in the 90s as I've been told. It was hardly any better in the early 2000s. The young and energetic young ladies working today need to know that we put up with a lot back then. Aside from the hectic job itself that will wear you out at a young age, it's about the people you encounter, upper-level management, corporate culture, and the culture of the people you serve. But we persevered as with those working in any other profession.

The presence of women pharmacists is the norm these days. High five to us all. Not giving in to discriminatory practices made it so that women in those work spaces became the norm. Aside from the difficulties all pharmacists complain about, I'd like to think that the way young women (especially Black women) are treated today is the result of the progression we forged from being present yesterday.

******

While working in Gwinnett Co. Georgia, a male technician who regularly worked during my shift got beside himself. I was cool with him and all the techs there for that matter. But I sometimes had a protective temperament towards him because he was openly gay. Now this was back in 2004 when gay men were not nearly as openly discriminated against as in years past but far from being accepted without incident in various environments including the workplace. I'll call him "Mickey." Mickey was tall and chubby. He was a fiery redhead inside and out with curious eyes and was arrogant as hell. I don't believe he had a single four-year degree but considered himself as informed and astute as a Professor of Omniscience at the prestigious Acumen University, all of which is as fabricated as his intellect. Although he may have enrolled there after earning a two-year certificate from Wikipedia Tech. I introduced him to my husband once. He looked at Ron like he wanted to put him on a plate and bite into his first taste of chocolate dessert. I was so tickled.

As overconfident as Mickey was, he would spout irrelevant facts during conversations at work. He was emotionally fragile but otherwise kind hearted. He once commented on the beautiful long well-kept hair of the Black women he saw at a church he visited. Looking at my split ends I knew what he was insinuating. I didn't have the heart to educate him on the evolution of weaves. It wasn't his biz anyway. He confessed to paganism and abhorred orthodox religion. He challenged the validity of the Holy Bible quoting some Greek philosopher about Old Testament content. I informed him that this philosopher wasn't nearly old enough to question the church's canon. Moreover, the NT was written in Kione Greek but the OT was written mostly in ancient Hebrew, a time long before Greek interpretation. With no brick to continue building his pagan ideology, he could only turn away to debate another day.

I think Mickey may have tried religion but was put off by anti-gay sentiment within the church. I just wish the message he heard was love. No one goes to church to be hated. They go there seeking love. It's all I ever showed him.

One pleasant afternoon Mickey was working at the register. A patient's mother was picking up a prescription for Clindamycin suspension. The mother asked him if it needed to be refrigerated. He said he believed it did. He then came over to ask me the same.

"No. Do not refrigerate that it will clump up in the bottle. Leave it at room temperature. Just be sure to shake the bottle before each dose." I told the mother.

This jackass says,

"Are you sure? Because I thought…"

He then proceeds to check the computer beside my verification terminal to look up the suspension to make sure I knew what I was talking about. He did it right in front of me! I looked at him as if he had lost his mind.

"Oh, I see. You're right."

I hold my peace while he reconstitutes the suspension granules of Clindamycin and completes the transaction. The mother leaves.

"Mickey don't ever do that again. Do not check the checker."

I said it twice in the kindest voice. I will not go on a rant as to how I knew he would not have done that to the older white pharmacists there. I'm merely pulling out a receipt.

******

At that same location a customer walked back to the pharmacy upset over his copay. Pointing at me he yelled,

"I'm a CPA and I will have your license taken for charging me this much for my medication!"

I was speaking with the senior technician when the *gentleman* came rushing back to the patient consult window with this accusation. I walked up to the computer next to the window. Then took a deep breath and began to type while being careful with my words.

"I didn't know a CPA could have my license taken away," I

sarcastically responded looking right at him still typing. "But I'll be happy to call your insurance company to find out why *they're* requiring you to pay so much."

I already knew why. He wanted the brand name. But having the audacity to threaten my pharmacy license like he had that kind of authority over me warranted going the extra mile for reproach. My senior tech, a young white male in his early 20s, sat by me in protective mode as he anticipated another routine moment of superiority complex syndrome. I used that moment to teach the tech what my former pharmacy manager in Louisiana taught me a few years earlier. Call the insurance company, echo everything the agent says. Watch the irate customer pick his face up off the floor. Win the moment as you watch the customer walk away in embarrassment. Turns out in this case the copay was supposed to be higher. I offered to change it. The man turned down the offer, ashamed, and left.

******

I made the mistake of getting into an argument with one of our regulars at the same site who got every medication one diagnosed with the trifecta (hypertension, diabetes, high cholesterol) could possibly have. We went toe-to-toe over test strips. He was attempting to pick them up but it was too early. Picking up testing supplies early is not an issue if a patient is paying the cash price. But this dark-chocolate 6'2" Santa Claus in coveralls was on Medicare and the CMS *don't play that*. Unfortunately for him, I had to deny the refill and give the date that his insurance will pay based on his testing frequency. I took the liberty of informing him that he could get it sooner if the prescriber increases the daily usage.

Otherwise, I told him he could get the test strips on a later date. He didn't like that. This is where the fight began.

I inquired, "Why are you out of test strips, Mr. Duncan? You should have plenty according to the doctor's directions."

He lied. He fussed, he yelled, he threatened, and he belittled. He even pounded on the pharmacy counter like a king demanding to be obeyed. I reacted and did not back down. This must have alarmed the senior tech who got in between the two of us suggesting that we run the test strips anyway under a 'change in testing frequency' override. The tech knows that I know the override exists. But it did not apply in this case. He was either over testing, sharing with someone else or wasting an expensive item that he did not have to pay for. Furthermore, we were audited more closely after that whole debacle where major pharmacy chains, including the one we worked for, were fined for violating federal reimbursement regulations. In other words, what the tech was doing was illegal. When it's caught and eventually it will be, the pharmacy loses reimbursement and we get a not-so-friendly email from our supervisor, who prior to, gets a not-so-friendly email from corporate. I didn't approve it. The senior tech gave it to the belligerent man anyway.

A couple of months or so later that long-time customer and I made up over the phone.

"I'm in Chicago." He informed me with that pleasant voice I knew before the verbal altercation.

I was actually thinking about him before the call, commenting to another tech that he hadn't visited the pharmacy in a while. He was living in Chicago for the summer.

"I own properteee!" He declared with pride about his home in the Midwest. He was filling his prescriptions there locally until he returned.

"Well, you are missed," I admitted as the sentiment was true. He'd been a customer there long before I began working at that site. He then confessed,

"My wife got on to me about what happened and she told me I needed to apologize."

He did. I did as well. All was forgiven and we lived to see another day. It was a moment of genuine repentance and mutual respect thanks to someone near and dear to him who knew what it was like to be me. I reveled in that moment of reconciliation until my next bout with my next irate customer.

******

I was working alone on a Saturday morning at that same wonderful location when a tall purple nosed white *gentleman* came in asking about the blood pressure machines. He was trying to decide which to buy. I compared the arm monitor to the wrist monitor.

"Which is more accurate?" He asked.

"The arm device with the automatic inflation is more accurate."

"What about the wrist one. I prefer that one. How inaccurate is it?"

"The wrist monitor has about a 3 to 5-point differential from the arm monitor."

I don't know if it was the expression on my face when I responded or if I appeared to be giving numbers from the top of my head. But he then acted like he was talking to an airhead teenager and began walking away as he disrespectfully responded,

"I don't think so and I don't think you know what you're talking about."

"I do know what I'm talking about," I said frowning and appalled. The nerve of this guy.

******

For the record, we took a crash course on blood pressure monitoring in pharmacy school. I remembered the nurse vividly who taught the class. I just don't remember her name. I'll refer to her as "Nurse Fun." She was a brown heavy lady with very short silver and gray hair. She was sarcastic and liked to crack jokes. She habitually pissed off one of my preceptors who spearheaded the clinical trial she was working on at the University. Nurse Fun had a reputation for practicing unprofessional decorum. She was just so entertaining to be around. We drove an elderly patient in the current trial to see a nationally renowned cardiologist near the lower 9th Ward because the patient's blood pressure was alarmingly elevated. The elderly woman seemed ill holding her head along the way. That is until a Nelly song came on the radio, *Hot in Herre*.

"That's my song!"

Her malaise magically disappeared. Waving her hands and gyrating in the backseat of the car.

"*It's getting hot in herre!*" She sang.

Nurse Fun was singing and gyrating along with her.

That fun nurse told me one day on another joyride that I should give to the panhandlers on the side of the road if they caught me at a stoplight.

"That could be Jesus asking for a dollar. I give it to them," she said.

Jesus is going to break a broke college student is all I could think of.

There were panhandlers at every other corner in New Orleans. I was a poor student. I believe Jesus knew my limitations. But it did prompt me to give more in the future.

Nurse Fun was methodical in her instruction and paid no mind to the impatient. She was my kind of people. Through her we learned the five beats that occur after pumping ceases so that the blood pressure monitor can detect an accurate blood pressure. The two that matter most are the first and last beats. That's your systolic and diastolic blood pressure. I remember learning the accuracies of the monitors and not to recommend the wrist monitor to patients unless they could not manage an arm cuff and monitor unit. It was an invention of convenience. I learned the same during a summer internship at UAMS in Little Rock, AR. I also remember the differential: +/- 3-5mmHg. This is mainly because the wrist cuff is more sensitive to body position. It was a helpful course. Nurse Fun was a good instructor.

******

I spent a long time upset over that encounter with the purple nose man. I'm talking years. Why would he say that? I played it over and over in my head. What I should've said. How I should've shown more confidence in what I said. Like it was me who did something wrong. I was making excuses for him. Giving validity to his blatant insult. There I was trying to help the first face at the counter that morning and that purple nosed man managed to turn that into a moment of regret.

'Sure sir. You can use the wrist cuff. It's just as good. Would you like to purchase here or do you have more shopping to do?'

It would have been a lie but I would have avoided the rudeness. I don't know why it bothered me for so long.

******

I was given a prescription for generic Percocet at the drive-thru one night. Same location. I kindly told the guy some information was missing on the script and I couldn't fill it. He leaves then comes back to the drive-thru.

"Sir I still can't fill this. It's missing necessary information." I give it back.

"Well, what's missing?! Why the hell can't you fill it?! I need this medicine."

"I need the doctor's DEA number and I will also need your ID," hoping he would give up at this point. He didn't.

He left. Then he came right back. The prescription now has a DEA number written on it. It just didn't belong to the doctor on the prescription. The DEA number didn't belong to any doctor, actually. It was a forgery. I suspected so when he gave it to me the first time. The guy would not go away. This time he came inside. Because it's harder to reject someone face to face without a glass barrier. Or so he thought.

"Sir, I cannot fill this prescription. It's forged," I said bluntly.

He snatched the prescription from my hand. There were some loud curse words he shouted expressing his disapproval. Then he yelled,

"This isn't over!"

"Are you threatening me?! Did you just threaten me?!" I yelled back. "Get out of here! Now!"

I cannot explain why, except that I was having an out of body experience but I took my glasses off and walked my petite self to the pharmacy door headed towards him, forehead first, as I was yelling back at him.

"Get out of here!"

My eyebrows were nearly touching my hairline and my eyes nearly bulging out of their sockets. You would have thought I was in the streets of Atlanta in full whoop-ass mode. I don't know what I was thinking. Thankfully he backed away while still yelling at me and left.

******

At a different location in the same county, I came in on a lonely weekend in a gloomy mood. It may have been because I just didn't want to be there. I don't quite recall. It was early in my career—the first location I was assigned to where I was interviewed. The location was suboptimal and the clientele was bleak. I wasn't crazy about management there either. The front end had a butthole of a manager. And the pharmacy had a manager, a Caribbean-American woman a few years older than me that I didn't necessarily vibe with but should've given more respect. At the time, it felt like I got the short stick as a new pharmacist.

Anyway, a Black lady probably in her forties came up to the drive-thru in a black car. She wore black sunglasses and a long, wavy black wig and black blouse with blue jeans. I said hello and asked for her information. I retrieved her medication. I sold it to her. With no questions asked. I said "thank you" and walked away. That wasn't the thing to do with this woman on this day. She sat there for a minute then drove off. About 5 minutes later the phone rang. It was her. Immediately screaming at me,

"I just wanted to tell you that was the worst service I have ever had!"

More screaming,

"I have never been treated that way and…!"

I'd go on but I think you get the picture. That lady put the fear of another Black woman in me. I put the phone on the counter and waited for the screaming to stop while I continued to work alone.

"Hello?!" She finally said.

I picked the phone back up.

"Yes?"

She said something then slammed the phone in my face. I must have made her feel as crappy as I was feeling. I have no clue as to how her morning began or how her week may have been just to end it with crappy service at a pharmacy drive-thru. Maybe I was PMSing. Maybe she was PMSing. I don't know. I do know that neither of us did the other any favors that morning. But it was all enough to bring me to tears. I could see one of the managers to the right at the far window in my periphery as I wiped my eyes but I didn't look at him. I wanted him to go away. He did. I looked up at the clock on the wall with tear-filled red eyes before I grabbed another prescription label. No more than 30 minutes had passed since I'd opened the shutters to begin my eight-hour shift alone.

******

My second pharmacy location in Gwinnett Co. Ga, before I began floating, was around 2005. The pharmacy was run by a might be, might not be true blonde female 10 years older than me. She was from Mississippi and oh so antebellum. I'm not being prejudice. The first question I recall her asking me was,

"What does your father do?"

"He works for a company that builds swimming pools. What does *your* father do?"

I don't remember what she said. I didn't really care. I did care why she felt comfortable asking me such a question. She just met me. Not that it was her biz but my father in totality did that and much more. My father owned and operated a laundromat, repaired appliances, air conditioners, water heaters, and HVACS. He repaired anything that broke around the house including the vehicles. He was a caregiver to his late blind mother for years, a husband, father and doting grandfather. I could have said all that but I didn't. Quite frankly, she didn't deserve to hear that or anything else my father did for a living. But the Southern belle does what she does. Judges. Classifies. Compares. Always considering the status quo the cream of the crop. The cream being well-off blue eyed and blonde-haired white women. Also, where you came from, where your family ended up and what daddy did for a living said all that one of her kind needed to hear about you. It's an old school way of thinking but a question still unabashed at that time. Needless to say, I could not stand her. Or maybe I need to say it. Getting old annoyances off your chest is cathartic you know. Tolerance for people like her by this company was so willfully accepted. Or perhaps the tolerance was on my part never having complained to HR about it. It triggered a sour stomach in me when encountering her type that did not soothe for years. I believe it was remedied the day I "set it off" on an elderly antebellum predecessor I worked opposite of at the Three Letter Pharmacy.

Nonetheless, I learned quite a bit from Mississippi's finest. She was good at her job. It would've been foolish of me to be there all that time and not watch and learn. We served mostly an upper middle class to wealthy clientele there. They ranged from kind to super entitled. I'd get questions like, "Angie what is Valtrex for?" Yelled from one end of the pharmacy to the other. Married men purchasing condoms. Or customers upset that we would dare to request a valid ID to purchase Sudafed and getting yelled at as a result. As I've demonstrated, it can be easy to lose your cool with some folk. But this pharmacist didn't. She pleased and she appeased a lot at a busy location, even when it seemed unreasonable. At first, I got the impression it all came easy as these people were probably her neighbors or within her community as she lived near there. That is until I witnessed one white female customer bring her to tears after insulting her. It was the first time I'd seen a pharmacist cry aside from myself. But even when an unruly person approached the counter or a mistake was made, she handled things with grace and humility, always making eye contact and appearing sincere.

When I finally thought about it, the previous female manager I worked with at my first location, who was from Jamaica, pleased and appeased her clientele just as well. She always did her best even though her location wasn't as hectic. I didn't particularly enjoy working alongside her either but her work ethic was identical to the blonde antebellum pharmacist. But I never credit it to her while being there beside her. I'm not for certain if it had to do with the volume or clientele that they served having been planted in noticeably different parts of the city. But it was regrettably easy to overlook the value of one pharmacy manager versus the other.

******

If karma is a thing, I certainly got mine on account of remaining in good graces with my old supervisors and abandoning female colleagues. I selfishly didn't think I needed to, as it appeared that most of the women I was acquainted with didn't necessarily get along with the supervisors in either district. I believed that lack of a good relationship with your boss meant never getting your way. What I did not consider was that our supervisor may have been apathetic towards the needs of some of the female employees. Things like rejecting time-off, being overwhelmed and not responding to emails for help, or ignoring complaints of disrespect that may have been gender or racially motivated. But if *I* had favor with an otherwise apathetic boss, that was good enough for me. Or so I thought.

After moving away from metro Atlanta and returning a few years later I sent an email as usual and got shifts at the snap of a finger upon my return. All good, right? Wrong. I thought it was odd that the scheduler kept contacting me to verify that I knew my welcome back shift would be in a city I hadn't worked in before. Upon my return in January 2011 I was navigated to an island called Rome, Ga to fill-in for another pharmacist. I'll spare the details about the environment there at that time and fast-forward to the snowstorm that landed the one day I worked there. Mind you, this is Georgia. Snow isn't common and snowstorms are almost non-existent. But for my lack of connection with the veteran pharmacists that I otherwise should've kept in contact with and consulted about the changes since I had left, would I have known to reject that shift. Not only was it a bad location, the district supervisor knew the storm was coming but gave me no warning in advance or while in transit.

Long story short, they made no reservations for me to stay overnight at a hotel which would have been required because of the hour-and-a-half commute. Neither did they provide emergency accommodations in the event I could not return home due to weather conditions. I had no idea what I was walking into until I was in it. The hotels were booked. The store I worked in closed early, but not before my shift began. All I could do was leave in the hope that I could return home in a 4-cylinder vehicle.

En route home, the snow was already accumulating fast. Inches high. I managed to drive behind a Mack truck in my little 2010 Corolla for 20 minutes or so once I made it to the long stretch of highway traveling southbound. The driver tracked about 5 minutes past a Walmart that appeared out of nowhere like a fixture in a snow globe after the fake snow settles. Then all of a sudden, he made a U-turn off the highway. The snow was just piling up too fast. He could no longer tread through it and visibility was minimal. What could I do but make a U-turn as well? He drove back to the Walmart. I drove back to the Walmart. We thought it might be open but no such luck. So, there we were along with about 10 other vehicles with drivers stuck in what was probably Georgia's first snowstorm in forever.

The mixture of ice and snow was still accumulating the longer we sat there. I called my husband soon after and sent him into a panic. I knew I wasn't going anywhere in the freezing cold and piling snow. I kept my car running with the heat to comfort me as long as possible without the threat of running out of gas. Then I had to turn the car off, fearing no gas station would be open the next day. We were at the very least going to be stranded there until morning. To make matters worse I left my phone charger at home. I talked to Ron intermittently as long as I could then had to hang up. The heat soon drifted out and the cold seeped in as it got darker. By nightfall I was effing freezing! Literally shivering with chattering teeth. Un-freaking-believable. I tried that mind over matter bull but could not escape reality. How ridiculous was this! How lousy was my district supervisor *and* the scheduler for that matter! No concern. No warning. No good deed goes unpunished. If only I had enough sense to keep in contact with my sister circle. Either one of them would have warned me for sure. I was stuck freezing my butt off in what seemed like the middle of nowhere. But so was everyone else around me. In the same abandoned snow-covered place—a Walmart parking lot. Everything we need on the inside of that superstore steps away and no one could get in. It reminded me of that Natalie Portman movie except we didn't have the luxury of being locked inside.

We all suffered the night's freezing temperatures. I slept in spurts bundled into my hooded coat with my arms wrapped around me. I was actually just grateful that matters weren't worse by the next day. What if that truck driver hadn't turned around and I hadn't followed? What if it snowed five times more than it did? What if I was alone and couldn't tolerate the freezing temperature? But none of that happened. For the most part, I was safe. I made it home 30 hours after I had left my driveway clueless.

7

TWA

From time to time, I come across a colleague that walks the line between arrogance and being downright rude. I'm sure some of my fellow pharmacists can relate. Like the one pharmacist who had no more than 2 years of experience but considered his management position as a thing of archaic superiority. At least he did the day I was there. He took over my verification station without asking and beyond workflow when he came in for the afternoon shift. I let it slide. I was courteous enough to help pull and fill prescriptions because we could both see his afternoon filling technician was a little slow. She mislabeled a prescription for Flonase that he thought I filled then flung the item across the counter to me while I was standing there counting pills. I looked at him like he'd lost his mind. He didn't have the nerve to make eye contact. I left it there and proceeded to count my last prescription at the filling station as his real tech returned from the drive-thru.

"That Flonase prescription he tossed over there is

mislabeled." I told her, pointing to it. "You can correct it if you want to. I'm not doin' it. I'm not a dog and I don't 'go fetch' for anything." I then walked over to the drive-thru.

I gave her a choice as to whether she should correct the error. I didn't think either of us were required to fetch anything tossed at us. Apparently, his royal highness thought otherwise.

******

Then there comes a time on occasion when floaters, like myself, cross paths with a lazy pharmacist or tech that assumes that the floater is unassuming to the point where we don't know our job, let alone theirs. So, they try me by sliding their work onto me. One time I suppose I was verifying prescriptions a little too quickly that I took a few moments to look at my phone. Then I went to the restroom. When I came back two stacks of prescriptions in filling baskets to be scanned and counted happened to have made their way right beside my terminal. I looked at the only possible suspect. Again, another culprit, not making eye contact. When I looked at the date for the label in the first basket it read, "Friday," with the ready-by-promise time. I asked,

"Are all these for tomorrow?"

"Yes. They are," the tech replied.

I politely slid the stacks back to the tech's slot. That location wasn't even busy enough for me to assume another pharmacist's work just so they can chill during the evening shift or the next day.

Then there's the occasional TWA, *Technicians With Attitudes*. As a seasoned employee of the female African American persuasion, I believe it is my obligation to school the Millennials and Gen Zs of the same category on professionalism when necessary. We have a few on/off switches we have to utilize when entering the workspace. One is language, two is tone, three is facial expression, four is savoir-faire. My favorite line of unsolicited advice is to tell her to '*check that sista girl at the door.*' That means leave the bad attitude and whatever kinda bad day you were having before you got to work at the door when you get to work. No one across that pharmacy counter cares about your personal life. Everyone across that pharmacy counter cares about your work life. To be fair though, unwelcoming attitudes among employees are more prevalent these days across racial lines and gender for multiple reason. But I used to pay more attention to those in the same category as me because I know the line we have to walk is super thin. We make a daily choice to wear the *yoke* or wear the *crown*. So, whether they welcome my words of wisdom or not, it was given during those years I worked full-time.

But back to the TWAs. I can tolerate self-absorption even arrogance on most days but I loathe a bad attitude. While they don't outweigh the good, I cannot count the number of times I've met those kinds of technicians in the pharmacy. I show them kindness. They show me their asses. That's when they get the speech. I find it especially interesting that a store level employee, whoever they are, can be that way. A TWA can show up for work every day as non-shareholders of the company they work for, but act like they own the joint. I mean really, they own nothing! Not their home, not their car, not their man or woman, not even a fraction of a share of the business that underpays them. Interesting. I imagine I'm not alone in my fact-of-life counseling in the workplace. I've even noticed Asian women giving staff the business at a few stops on the pharmacy trail. I don't think it's racist to say that Korean American female pharmacists that I've met seem to be the least tolerant of bull or being bossed around behind the pharmacy counter. And then some technicians are just passive aggressive for no good reason. Wicked behavior wrapped in warm smiles.

Nonetheless, I've only had one tech get under my skin to the point where I dismissed her. I told her she could leave the pharmacy. She stayed. I guess unpaid bills superseded her bad attitude that day. She chose not to say a word to me thereafter and did her job, albeit begrudgingly. As one who is typically unfazed by any rude, insubordinate individual, it takes an exceptional amount of asinine to get to me. That troll did it. I'll leave it at that.

******

While working in Richmond County, I was verifying what was supposed to be Amlodipine, a blood pressure medicine, gathered from a dispensing cell. Except upon looking at the image of the pill on the verification screen I can see that it's not the pill in my possession. It's similar. But not the right one. So, I returned it to the filling technicians to redo.

"This isn't Amlodipine." I kindly told them. I reach for the next prescription in the next tote.

It was given back five prescriptions later. I open the

prescription bottle and pour a few of the round pills in the child-protective top to get a closer look.

"These are not the right tablets." I repeated (I wasn't making a suggestion). I look at them. No reciprocating eye contact. Just fast-paced movement getting prescriptions toted. No response. But at least I know they heard me. No problem.

I'm still observing them as I simply place the item in its tote and return it yet again. The techs are hustling as expected for this time of the day. Pulling labels, scanning, counting, bottling, toting, then passing them down the river to the pharmacist's station. Neither of them turned my way.

There's a reasonable line between a simple error and blatant disrespect. One can be overlooked, the other not so much. I learned by this time to not allow emotions to get the best of me. If I lose a job it won't be because I was the angry Black lady that no one could stand to be in the same room with. It would be on my own recognizance. When I stopped loving what I did for a living, I'd quit. Dignity intact. The old Angie might react to blatant insubordination or rude customers. But not refurbished Angie. I smiled more, laughed more and did not wear my feelings on my sleeve. It took a lot to shake me and even more to make me raise my voice by that time. Even when clearly being tested. But this? This was overt disrespect. Would you believe that without uttering a single word these passive aggressive witches gave me the same tote with the same drug a third time? I earnestly laid the old Angie to rest nearly a decade ago...but these disrespectful females would rather have me resurrect that *bitch*.

I sign off of the computer, which basically shuts down

pharmacy operations, rendering everyone useless. Remove my old lady glasses, turn my back to anyone who may have been standing on the other side of the counter to be served and yelled like I was addressing a classroom of disobedient five-year old kids:

"I don't know what this crap is but it's not Amlodipine! Pull the cell and show me the bottle it came from! This is not the right drug!"

Why do I have to yell at these heifers? Why keep giving me the same pills?! Because those pills were in cell #5. Cell #5 says "Amlodipine" and the label says "Amlodipine #5". Ergo, whatever's in cell #5 has to be Amlodipine. Except it wasn't. It was Amitriptyline. Same manufacturer. Same kind of bottle. Same shape. Same markings. Different color. Wrong cell.

"Empty the cell and find the right bottle! Check the computer to see if any more were filled from that cell." I signed back on to the computer temper flared.

Not another word was said.

Upon returning the next day, I learned that the overnight pharmacist poured the tablets from the wrong 500 count bottle into cell #5. Both came in the same big blue sized bottle by the same manufacturer with nearly identical labels. That mistake was way too easy to make. She never had help at night. She must've had one hectic shift working alone the night before. Those cells were soon updated to robots that required initials, imaging and scanning before filling any slots. It was an expensive and necessary upgrade.

******

I met one TWA while working in South Atlanta. It goes
without saying that the AM shift should have an AM attitude.
This technician did not. We didn't know each other upon
meeting that morning but she made it clear that I was not the
pharmacist she wanted to see. Not even a partial grin, but an
'*Ima bout to fight somebody*' grimace. I remember thinking
almost immediately that she looked familiar. However, I
admit to being the type that thinks she knows every other
black person she meets. The tech made it a point to be cold. I
made an equal effort to be warm. She was just as cold and dry
with the customers. Under the circumstances, not having
another tech to switch with her in case she got pissed for
being reprimanded, I didn't bother to correct her. I'm just a
visitor. The location was in a Black neighborhood, a mix
from poor to wealthy. Some well-known African Americans
live in the area. There's also a megachurch nearby, Elizabeth
Baptist Church, where my husband and I were once
members. A piece of the Black Mecca. Which begged the
question, "Why walk through the door like you're here to
serve your enemy?" Do you know where you are?

The rest of the day's crew trickled in. As the day went by, I
kept telling myself I'd seen the mean technician before, still
not convinced otherwise. The afternoon pharmacist strolled in
around 2pm. He may have been the manager. I don't know.
African American male pharmacists were like unicorns.
You'd remember each one because you could count them on
one hand. Plenty of African men, Caucasian, Arab and
Pacific Asian men, but hardly any *bruthas*. I say that
facetiously.

It was quite busy as expected. The rest of the staff were friendly. The general mood there was whatever we're talking about comes 1st and serving these customers comes 2nd. I'm just a visitor. It was just an observation at that location in that piece of the Mecca.

By the end of my shift my memory returned in full. Turns out I actually had seen the mean technician before.

"Did you go to Central High? Do you know my brother, Macon?"

"I went to Central." She said slightly surprised but in agreement. "I graduated in '99."

"Then you should know my cousin, MeMe. Weren't you a cheerleader?"

My cloudy memory became clear. She was indeed a cheerleader at our high school six hours away and over a decade earlier. I played basketball which meant we rode the bus together during away games. She was a friend of my cousin who was also a cheerleader at that time. We finally exchanged pleasantries after being in the same space for 8 hours. She was a homegirl. Whaddayaknow. I captured an elusive smile from her as I exited through the door.

8

Emulsions Can Be Deceiving

Sometimes people or even our professions are not as they seem. They're like emulsions—an illusion of stability. The emulsion wears a cover. But underneath, it's actually an incohesive mess pretending to be something it's not. As it pertains to people, we can be fooled by first appearances, pleasantries, and professional decorum. Soon enough, though, the content of one's character surfaces revealing who they truly are. As far as our professions, once the cover is blown, the reality of what we signed up for can turn out to be a devastating blow.

******

There were plenty of pharmacy robberies to speak of in Georgia and nationwide for that matter. But I would be remiss if I didn't give just as much attention to incidents of theft that were completely in-house. For example, I worked at one location north of Atlanta where I was told by the pharmacy manager that one of our techs had been fired while

I was on maternity leave. The guy had the nerve to steal Viagra. It was only available in brand name at the time. It was also treated like CII meds. Pharmacies stocked it alongside opioids in a safe or locked cabinet where only the pharmacist had a code or key to access it. I didn't ask how he did it. I just lingered mentally on how I just could not believe this kind-hearted technician was capable of such a thing. But he was.

******

During my first internship with Wrong-Aid Pharmacy in Madison County near Memphis, TN, I overheard the pharmacy supervisor speaking with the pharmacy manager. They were discussing an injection used for cancer patients that came up missing from the fridge. I don't remember the name of the drug but I do recall that it was expensive. The supervisor shared with the manager that his partner, who had sold his independent pharmacy to the big chain we were working for, informed him some time ago that his wife had cancer and was undergoing treatment. I don't know if they got to the bottom of it, but it's no secret that independent owners drew their lines of violations far beyond that of a major drug chain.

******

While in pharmacy school I had a classmate who was quite loquacious but super friendly. So I conversed with them from time to time. They were wide-eyed and wore a bright smile daily. I admired their enthusiasm and energy. My classmate did not necessarily dress to impress like a typical Xavierite. Their day-to-day attire was a bit sloppy. But one could easily chalk that up to life as a full-time student, parent and part-time pharmacy employee. Who had the time to worry about appearances? I was guilty of self-neglect and bad breath myself on occasion. We weren't friends but they were always good for a conversation. I remember how my classmate always sat in the front of the class. They were attentive and asserted themselves noticeably. If we weren't all in a doctoral program, I would've labeled them a super nerd for exerting so much interest about disease states, how drugs work and other particularities of pharmacotherapy.

To be fair though, the one thing all pharmacy students have in common is an affinity to understand how things work to make a difference, their mechanism of action (MOA). Specifically, the mechanism of action of drugs. All drugs are manufactured with a purpose in mind. What's their purpose? How are they useful? What makes them do what they do? What makes them appropriate for a particular disease state, or for a particular kind of pain. What causes them to fail? What side effects or adverse effects are they capable of? What happens if they are abused?

How is it that a medication can get FDA approval now and cause havoc on a patient's body years later? Like Zantac possibly causing cancer 20 years after it hit the market. Are you kidding me?! A drug that keeps me from burping up stomach acid can induce colon cancer?! How is it that something designed to make you feel better could make you feel worse? It's an anomaly. That is until you get to the core of its consciousness. NDMA, an environmental contaminant found in many medications, food and water, is a source of misery that hides under the radar. In small amounts it's harmless to humans. But in the case with Zantac (ranitidine), it was revealed in an independent study that harmful amounts of NDMA resulted taken by mouth. It possibly mixes with stomach acids and produces more NDMA producing toxic levels. Metformin ER and previously Valsartan, were under scrutiny as well. Valsartan and Zantac (ranitidine) [not to be confused with Zantac 360 (famotidine)] were both recalled by the FDA. As I said before drugs are anomalous. There's nothing simplistic about them. How they work when put to the test is just as profound and complex as the actions of human beings. It's all fascinating.

But back to my classmate. A person you could've easily given a side eye of annoyance, was just too polite not to like. At the very least you had to be nice to them, even on the day when the shit hit the fan for them. The pharmacy walls had ears and everyone was talking about it. "Sammy Sunshine" was stealing OxyContin from the pharmacy where they worked. Not a few tablets here and there, mind you, but bottles of 100 count OxyContin. How could someone so smart and jolly do something so stupid and felonious? I was shocked as were many other classmates. *"How?,"* really was the question. We found out they were entrusted with checking in schedule II orders for the staff pharmacists. Those orders would include Adderall, Methadone, Oxy, etc. Technology wasn't so great back then. Quantities could easily be manipulated with a click and a pen. On a computer an order for 4 OxyContin bottles can magically become a 3. On paper, 3s can become 2s. Sevens can become 1s or vice versa. Otherwise, pharmacy managers and staff were just way too lax about keeping inventory. Yeah, it was that simple. "Pat the Perpetrator" claimed someone close to them made them do it. I didn't know how to respond to that except to give them a well-deserved side eye followed by my best sister girl eye roll. Quite frankly I couldn't get past the facade they displayed everyday as the perfect student—how calculating they were.

That happened to be my first lesson in core consciousness, but as it pertained to people. Some people, like those drugs mentioned, are not who they pretend to be. Deceitful by nature. Not an error, an isolated poor decision or momentary misjudgment. I'm talking lifestyle. There doesn't need to be a personal attack against you or another individual. Rather, this is raising an alarm on how some people think and move while no one's looking. I've learned to practice discernment. It's not a crime to keep your distance from deceitful people. From that point on, I merely smiled when walking past my classmate, if they bothered to make eye contact. Otherwise, I never spoke to them again.

******

Kindness is of the essence. The Bible says that *God resists the proud, But, shows grace to the humble* (James 4:6). Everyone experiences both. We need only practice one. Depending on the nature of the matter, when I encounter a prideful person, a self-centered person and even an arrogant person at work, I simply give them what they want—validation. If they over explain as if I just walked into a pharmacy for the first time, I let them explain. If they offer intel on the bad employees, while assuming they are the good employee, I offer my attention. If they run to particular customers because they believe I lack the experience to handle that special individual with their individual needs, I let them run. It's their territory. If they offer unsolicited advice, I listen. If they want to pretend to be the boss, be that. If they try to finagle their work onto me or make me the object of lies, well, that's where I draw the line. I'd advise anyone in any professional environment to be extra cautious of deceitful colleagues. Like the ones who will attempt to hide their irreparable errors or misfills. Or perhaps you have worked with those who will throw you under the bus and even lie to save their own behinds. Sure, you've met them.

It just so happens that the company I worked for the least appeared to come with the most deceitful employees. I have never met so many lying pharmacists than with the Three Letter Pharmacy drug store chain. Although it should be taken into account that I only worked in one area south of Atlanta for that company in the community setting.

My introduction was a pharmacy manager lying to a member of the state Board of Pharmacy about my immunization status for the zoning district. As usual I moved and had to get yet another notarized document for my current immunizing location. It's something totally unnecessary as if a healthcare worker's immunization capabilities magically disappear by working in another district. But the document was required by the state per district at the time. Alternatively, one affidavit is needed that included all the districts or counties where the pharmacist administers shots. Mine was not on file at my current worksite because I forgot to get it for the umpteenth time. I float. It happens. I would need an affidavit with all 159 counties to satisfy the law. And of course, the inspecting agent has to find something wrong or their job would not be worth its existence.

"Yes, she has it. I'll let her know to bring a copy here to be kept on file."

The manager said something of that fabricated nature knowing I had just started there but could not turn people away who wanted to get flu shots or other immunizations. They told me the next day about the unannounced visit and what they told the board member as if they'd had saved my butt. But I know better. They were saving their own butt as the PIC (pharmacist in charge). The PIC is responsible for making sure their assigned location is in compliance with federal and state laws. It involves a lot of dotting "i's" and crossing "t's." But they signed up for the role. So, I don't have a lot of pity to that degree for the position. They were young and I imagine as a manager, thinking on their feet meant to apply false truths where needed. But why lie? A safe and appropriate response would have been to apologize that the document wasn't there and that they would contact me to clarify that a copy would be needed on site. A little dancing. No lies. Of course, I say all this not having been put in the same position.

I found out they and other pharmacists would fabricate KPIs for consumer calls. KPIs are statistics used to determine if a location is meeting company goals. We were required to follow up on newly prescribed medications, late refills and medication therapy management. On an average day it was difficult if not impossible to meet daily goals for customer care calls. This was realized when a part-time pharmacist or floater was on duty. However, we, the part-time pharmacists/floater, would get lower scores than full-time staff members because they were being dishonest about customer interaction for those metrics.

For instance, a pharmacy manager might call someone's residence and get no answer but would record the call as having contacted and counseled the patient. That of course was a lie because the patient never picked up the phone. Alternatively, if the actual "no response" is recorded then the call is cycled back through as incomplete and thus scored negatively. If everyone would just be honest, the company would have no choice but to withdraw from unrealistic goals or change the metrics to achieve those goals. The imbalance of when the manager records a call as "completed" vs. "not completed" as opposed to when an honest floater or part-time pharmacist is there, causes unwarranted scrutiny.

I received a phone call after work from my manager at that location explaining to me that '*what we do is...*' They all but admitted to the game. I told them that I was a team player and would fall in line. Ultimately, I didn't. I later quit. That experience plus a myriad of others weighs on the conscience. We have to answer to Someone much greater than corporate execs when this is all over.

Pharmacists or any healthcare professional for that matter have no business being in the business if we lose sight of who and why we serve. Successful statistics are always secondary to service no matter what management or district supervisors or corporate execs say. For instance, not getting in contact with a patient who's missed two weeks of his warfarin refill, who we claimed to have spoken to but didn't, who soon after suffered a stroke is a casualty of our negligence. I'd caution every healthcare professional especially pharmacists to be more concerned about having to answer for what we did for those we were assigned to serve rather than what KPIs we satisfied.

******

Another rookie pharmacist who prematurely acquired the PIC position reported a dispensing error to my culpability. Only the incident spurred from his carelessness of not knowing how to calculate an appropriate quantity for a diabetes injection pen, Victoza. The wrong unit was ordered the day prior to my shift. Upon receiving it to be dispensed, I noticed they hadn't ordered the right one. I printed the product screen and had the tech order the appropriate unit. The note politely warned the pharmacist who was to come in the following day (who I knew would be the manager) to be careful with the dosing which may change per patient and to be sure to dispense the appropriate quantity the next day. Less than a week later, I see a dispensing error report gifted to me. It's the Victoza. What and how? So I investigated only to find that not only was the original prescription never updated to the appropriate amount but the note I left was ignored. This means, my friends, that without any correction and scanning on the day the drug was dispensed, that the previous scan and label of the Victoza (under my name, because the ordered product was scanned during my shift) would have contained a label with my initials on it even though it left the pharmacy verified by another pharmacist. So who gets blamed for a stupid miscalculation that my 10-year-old son at the time could have figured out? Me! But, the nail in the coffin was the lie. It always comes back to the lie. The patient must've noticed the mistake and brought it back. But the dishonest rookie manager reports the incident as if I was responsible for the error. Believe me, as I've confessed, I can screw up all on my own. I don't need a sidekick. But to pretend on an official report as if they weren't the culprit? I was floored. What harm is it to hold yourself accountable? We don't typically lose our jobs over errors. We *can* lose our jobs by lying or over a cover up. I found out from time to time that some errors weren't being reported at all at some locations.

Integrity matters. The healthcare business is not the place to lose it. I hate to have ever had to report my own error. I hate even more to have to report someone else's. But if we neglect to do so, corrective measures are not made and it could cost someone, namely the patient a lot more than our bruised ego.

******

The last lying pharmacist I worked opposite of with that company was also a manager. I'll refer to them as "Terry" in a town 20 miles or so outside of Atlanta. If you've lived in Atlanta long enough you know that distance (20+miles) is culturally significant. This person was a special kind of pharmacist. One would otherwise think should have been retired. They were paying for private school for their grandkids in metro Atlanta. As it turns out, according to them, there were too many immigrant Hispanics at the nearby public school who couldn't speak English and were slowing down the classes to their grandkids' dismay. As a parent who has children schooled in metro Atlanta who's well aware of the accommodations made for Spanish speaking students, whose children were also enrolled in honors and AP courses, I couldn't help but think, *maybe it's not the Hispanics slowing your grandchildren down.* Yeah, Terry was a classic kind of old school Georgia pharmacist. The deep-fried Southern kind, unaware or unwilling to accept that their way of thinking was not so welcome anymore. As one of the techs summed it up,

"If it was up to Terry, their staff pharmacist would be 'blonde hair and blue eyed.'"

A younger version of them, I presumed...

Well, one evening during the flu season, Terry calls me on my way home after my shift. We worked inside of a super store where the pharmacy division was acquired by the Three Letter Pharmacy. The operating hours were shorter than a corner location so we never overlapped or saw each other. Our shifts were always separate. Terry called me in reference to our stats with the flu shots. Flu shot goals are a huge deal with major retailers. The manager wanted me and the tech that worked with me to do better to meet those goals.

"Sure, better we'll do. Talk to you later, Terry."

That's the way I remember it anyway. What I definitely remember is not making any comments about the tech I worked with. The next day on a lovely Saturday I open the pharmacy just before 9am, ice coffee in my hand. My tech, Janet, shows up an hour later on schedule. I speak to her. She gives me a dry,

"Hi."

I shrug it off, chalking it up to her preferring to be at home enjoying the weekend with her kids and boyfriend. No harm there. I talk her ear off as usual. But then I realized that there was no reciprocating convo. I look at her but there's no eye contact. *Ok, now I know something's wrong*, I thought. But I'm sensitive to people's personalities. This tech will tell you if she wants you to know something. Janet was a Caucasian sister girl. She was cool. The other tech, Renée, who happens to be of the same persuasion was cool too but whined a bit. On any given day I could expect a contorted expression followed by an immature, "I don't like this," in a Southern drawl. I'd smile in response as her signature complaining was cute, yet juvenile. The two made a good team. Both techs were 30-something year old moms that lived nearby. Both gave great customer service on any day. Except this day the sister girl tech had an at-ti-tude. I let it ride until she was ready to spill it. After snatching about 20 prescription labels from the printer and 20 drugs from the shelves, she turns towards me and aired her grievance,

"Did you tell Terry I wasn't trying to help get flu shots?!"

"What?!" I responded in disbelief.

"Terry said you said that I wasn't helping meet our flu shot goal!" Janet told me.

"No, I did not! Terry told you that?! First of all, they called me on my way home which I hate because I'm off the clock. Second, there was no conversation about you except that I assured them we would do our best. Third, why would I be concerned about the flu shot goal?! I do NOT get a bonus! I get a shout out from the district supervisor via GroupMe! That's why you've been in a funk? I would have never caused a wedge between me and a technician I have to work with and depend on. Why would they say that?! They're not getting away with that." I shook my head. "I'm calling Terry right now."

The call:

"Hello."

"Terry, this is Angie. Did you tell Janet that I said she wasn't helping me meet our flu shot goal?!"

"Well, she isn't. [bs, bs and more bs]," I was told during the call.

"I didn't say anything about Janet. *You* called me complaining about our current stats. [something, something, something...]."

Now at this point Terry hangs up in my face. However, their testimony was that they were in a super store, not the one I'm working in, and the call dropped. It didn't matter. I had no problem with calling them right back to commence checking them on their bullshit. I could not believe they flat out lied on me! I called Terry on their day off and handled it the way I did because it needed to be nipped in the bud so I could continue to talk Janet's ear off without the aura of bitchness in the air. But I also wanted to make it clear with Janet that the person she's been conversing with, sharing her personal life and experiences with, was not someone who would belittle her efforts when I leave the pharmacy. And she should know that I would never speak negatively about her behind her back. I am with her as I am with all other pharmacy sisters. *I'll say it to your face!*

The manager told a cowardly lie and would not fess up. I must have stunned them, calling to yell at them on *their* Saturday off. (They tried to return the favor out of spite on another day, quibbling over the phone about something I left in the pharmacy that was supposed to be mailed. I laughed about it; knowing Terry was making a mountain out of a molehill. So petty.) And yes, I was ok with bothering them on that day off as they did me after I clocked out for the day. But then it hit me why they may have waited until after my 10-hour shift. Terry didn't want to talk while Janet was with me at the pharmacy. Because Janet would've heard every word I said without conflict. What a manipulative thing to do. I hadn't worked there very long. No staff pharmacist had. That manager had 3 partners in 4 years. I was number 4 and the longest to survive. The one after me didn't last a year.

Terry knew that Janet would believe their every word. What they didn't know is that Janet had a little *sista* girl in her too. *Ima ask you to your face.* I'm glad she did. If there was any trust between myself and Terry, it was lost that day.

******

I did like both techs while working there. Had I stayed longer, we all might have been friends. Even as one of them, the sister girl, had a niche for saying what was on her mind without reservation.

Speaking of which, we were discussing whatever on another random day when the conversation pivoted to the movie, *Black Panther*, released in 2018. You would have to be in a coma to not want to see this highly anticipated movie co-written by the young and super talented director Ryan Coogler. I had a few customers that made it known that they were going to see it or had already seen it. One customer, who loved wearing a baseball cap when he came in, and loved calling me "queen," and loved spitting Black philosophy, and looked so handsome when he finally took that cap off while wearing his Sunday best, commented to me,

"Have you gone to see it?"

"Not yet. We're going on Sunday," I responded.

"Yeah. It was good. But check your ticket stub though. They been switching tickets," he informed me.

"Oh yeah?"

"Yep. Tryna stump ticket sales," he said assuredly. "Support Black actors."

"I can't wait to see it." I told him.

I smiled, resuming my work as he walked away, shaking my head at his current cute conspiracy theory.

Janet in protest mode, proclaimed that she and her boyfriend were not going to see the movie. I looked at her in a '*I can't wait to hear this one*' kinda way.

"I heard it's racist."

She stated this while still filling prescriptions, never once turning her head to look at me eye to eye.

"Really? How so?"

"My boyfriend said they made references to white people as 'colonizers.'"

"Colonizers?" I asked.

"Yeah!" We're not going to see it if it's a racist movie."

"So, you two are going to be the only ones not going to see

97

Black Panther because you heard it's racist."

"Yep," she nodded, still grabbing labels and counting tablets by 5s.

"You know it's a movie. It's not real," I told her.

"Mmmhmm," she nodded. Needing to get something from her side of the pharmacy, I walk her way,

"Wakanda is an imaginary escape for 2 hours and 15 minutes where Black people get to be themselves, see themselves, save themselves without consequence. And everybody, including white viewers get to enjoy it."

"Mmmhmm," she nodded again with pursed lips.

I get what I need from the counter and stand facing her never getting her eyes to address mine,

"And when it's aaallll over," I said, "you get to walk out of that theater and go back to the real world….and so do we. So, for 3 hours including previews and credits—eat it."

I witnessed a cynical grin and nod as she never missed a beat folding those labels and emptying those pills into those bottles. There was an awkward silence for about 60 seconds before I asked,

"So how are your kids?"

EMULSIONS CAN BE DECEIVING

PART II: THE LEARNING CURVE

9

Compounding Interest

While I'm on the subject of race matters, I want to draw attention again to Madison County, TN. An area near Memphis where I felt welcomed and unwelcomed all at the same time. It was where I first interned in 2000 as a pharmacy student at Wrong Aid Pharmacy. It was also an eye-opening experience to what I perceived as pure hatred. Up to that point I had only witnessed blatant racism once as a child that I can recall.

******

That first racial gut-punching experience was in 2nd grade when a group of girls and myself from our Project Discover class were playing together at recess. There were 6 to 8 of us, mostly Black girls and one Chinese American girl, Stacey. She was the minority of minorities. Her hair was just under shoulder length, a bob I suppose, and it flopped whenever she ran. She smiled a lot and was very friendly, a sweetie pie. Along with the rest of us, she had a lot of fun within our group during recess. The thought of race never entered our young and impressionable minds. Until that inevitable day came. A white classmate, Lisa, pulled our smiley-face friend aside while we were playing and whispered something in her ear. We were unmoved by the interruption so as to not cease having fun during our timed break. But then someone noticed that our friend didn't return to the group. We all then stopped and saw her from afar. She was playing with her "new friend." Well, we went over as concerned as we were and asked her why she didn't come back to play with us.

That moment was so vivid that I actually remember the two girls' faces, their expressions and exactly where we all were standing. I still remember their voices and even what they were wearing that day on the playground. Stacey, the Chinese girl, wore a white short-sleeved shirt with pink hearts and pink pants. Lisa, the white girl, wore a dark blue jean jacket, gathered at the shoulder, a white shirt and khaki pants. I was probably wearing burgundy corduroys and a Disney shirt. With the most innocent smile, Stacey told us what Lisa said to her.

"She told me that if I keep playing with you that I would turn black."

Everybody froze. Our eyes and mouths couldn't get any wider. We were so stunned looking at each other. Then we looked at Stacey and eventually pierced our eyes in the direction of the culprit. Prior to that moment I would otherwise say that we were oblivious to thoughts of race and understandably so at ages 7 and 8.

"You'll turn black?!" We all retorted in unison.

We had never heard anything like that before. Understand hearing this in the 2nd grade. We were unknowing kids at play until that moment. Now a portion of our innocence was stolen.

It's cathartic to speak about it now. I don't think any of us in our group knew what racism was but we knew an insult when we heard one. I'd never heard the word "black" or Black people used as a pejorative that I could remember. Plus, I hadn't seen *Roots* yet. Lisa had insulted us to our friend. Air had left our bodies. Or at least it had left mine. It wasn't the word "nigger" (I didn't know that word at that age) but it may as well have been considering the intent. At that age we had been punched in the gut by a peer armed with a proverbial racist fist. She isolated Stacey and in a matter of seconds, she turned our friend against us.

I imagine Lisa's hateful transition happened the same way at home. Thinking back on that day, I cannot comprehend how a parent who is not Black, who has children who are not Black could consciously prejudice their child against classmates who were mostly Black. I find it difficult to believe that a 7-year-old could conjure up negative thoughts that are specific toward a particular people without adult influence. Who else could Lisa have learned such hate from, let alone have the audacity to share it while at school? It wasn't natural for a kid. She knew it was wrong having injected her hate as a whisper into our friend's ear. It took effort to do that.

Lisa's teacher, Mrs. Price, was Black. The majority of her classmates were Black. In our hometown in Phillips County, AR, she was likely to have a Black neighbor. And that's what she'd been thinking of us all that time? I knew of no such perception until Lisa introduced it to me. Although it would explain her proclivity to distance herself in the classroom. At 7 and 8 years old we would never have known how to identify her kind of behavior. But like generations before us, like generations after, we learn hate early. We also learn the impact of hate.

We took our naive friend back. Then went and told our teacher what Lisa said before recess ended. Mrs. Price was livid. I don't recall how the matter was handled but I know I never looked at Lisa the same again. She disappeared after 2nd grade. Or perhaps she just became invisible to me after that year.

******

But back to the not-so-distant past in Madison County, TN. This is the place where the adventures of retail pharmacy began for me. What was uncommon became common. And the abnormal was normal. If an elderly woman came to the pharmacy counter asking,

"How do you get milk out of a man's breast?" Don't be surprised. It's Madison Co.

And… if another elderly woman calls the pharmacy complaining that her KY jelly tastes funny on her toast, just kindly remind her that slippery translucent stuff does not go in her mouth. It's to help her smoothly insert her catheter in her pee hole.

"Sippin' on Sizzurp" was the latest way to get high and your nearest pharmacy had the supply. The trend was just getting heavy when we noticed an unhealthy number of prescriptions for Tussionex being handed to us at the pharmacy counter and drive-thru. Little by little we began to reject them. One black guy who realized he wasn't going to fool us anymore began sending his polite and petite white girlfriend inside to drop off the prescription. Then she would pick it up later with a pearly smile,

"Thank you, guys!" Effortless.

We later caught on to the scheme and dismissed her too.

The pharmacy staff there was a smorgasbord of cultures. One tech was Jamaican. She could not stand the other two loud and talkative Southern fried African American techs who should've been mother and daughter 15 years separated considering how much they conversed with each other. "Girl" this and "chile" that. A young African American pharmacy manager ran the place. An older white staff pharmacist who didn't mind letting one rip from time to time worked opposite of him. He was the former independent pharmacist that sold his business to the chain pharmacy. On occasion, a 22-year-old hyperactive Chinese American floater pharmacist zipped through. He said he only slept 2 hours a day. I could've sworn he was on some quality cocaine. He never let a patient leave the pharmacy without being counseled on a new prescription. I liked that about him. There was a Black female extern native to the area, but she only showed up when she felt like it. And then there was little ol' skinny, dark and lovely me with a crinkled bob and bangs for the summer working there as an intern.

It was pretty cool to have such a diverse representation behind the counter. But I suppose having so many people in the pharmacy made the pharmacy manager somewhat paranoid. Especially since an expensive medication disappeared under his watch.

We were busy one day but I paused in effort to disappear to the back of the pharmacy. Seconds later I see the manager peaking back there to see what I was up to. We both burst into laughter as he caught me taking a huge bite into my 2nd or 3rd vanilla cupcake that the extern had baked for the staff. I hated not being trusted but I understood that he had a responsibility to monitor everyone, including me.

******

The tide had turned drastically for the profession on the cusps of the year 2000. And oh, how it made the good ol' boys flesh turn from pink to red. The bad taste in their mouths wasn't so overt as it was nuanced. The store manager there at Wrong-Aid was a peculiar pink guy. I'm not exaggerating. He had pink skin. His stiff-necked hellos were meshed into smiles that were too wide for the greeting. He would only seem to make appearances at the pharmacy when the pharmacy manager wasn't there. The pharmacy manager as I mentioned was a black guy in his early thirties. His partner, the staff pharmacist, was a white fellow in his mid-sixties. Right around the same age as the store manager. The store manager would make these comments to the staff pharmacist that were borderline offensive. He'd make contemptuous remarks that included "them" and "us."

A twenty-something year old white store employee worked the day shift there regularly. He was a dark, long-haired guy, thin and lanky, about medium height. He never smiled but spoke to us often in the pharmacy. One day he was sweeping the floor when a pharmacy tech asked him where the store manager was. He told her,

"Probably at a Klan meeting."

He was kidding but not kidding, you know? I found out soon after that the store manager would make numerous racist comments to that same employee not realizing that the young man was disgusted by his duplicitous conversations. He was fired before the end of my summer internship. But that was just the tip of the iceberg.

Elderly white men would frequent the store to pick up prescriptions and converse with the staff pharmacist; many of whom seemed to have a previous relationship with him from his old pharmacy. They openly expressed their disapproval with the "change" and how things were so "different." Again, you could hear the references of "them" and "us." All of this of course could have been shrugged off as being misunderstood if what happened during my shift one day hadn't happened.

A disabled man who happened to be Black came in the store and headed for the pharmacy. His legs were bent inward to the knees then outward to his feet. Imagine the worst case of knock knees that would require crutches. He looked like he could tip over any minute. Two of our usual elderly white male customers were near the pharmacy ahead of him a few feet away talking to one another as they waited for their prescriptions. The disabled man was just a few steps away from the pharmacy when he lost his balance and began to fall. The oldest tech and I saw him and ran towards the counter.

The tech shouted,

"Oh Lord! Catch him! Catch him!"

One of the two men whose back was towards the falling customer casually turned his head to witness the event as the helpless man tried unsuccessfully to grab an end stand only to land on the hard gray-speckled tile floor. The observer's compadre tilted his head to see. My tech and I came around as fast as we could as we saw that he wasn't going to regain his balance. All we could do was help him up. He was a tall man well over 6 ft. beyond 200lbs. We really had no business trying to lift him nearly dead weight. But it's a reaction when you see someone fall right? It's natural. If you can, you come to their rescue. If you see someone in trouble, you do something. While coming around the counter and through the pharmacy door, we both saw the two men who looked at the fallen customer with no urgency or concern, turn their heads back towards each other and continue their conversation. The tech was so upset she lost her composure. The one who was resting his left arm on a 5 ft. tall snack stand never moved. It was as if they both saw nothing. Didn't lend a hand. Didn't ask if he was ok. Their feet were planted. That wasn't a natural response. It was hateful. It was the one and only summer internship I spent in Madison County, TN. I imagine things are different now. I couldn't say for sure. I never went near that place again.

Counterfeit: They Sold It. We Bought It

I decided to write this book in part to expose experiences within this profession that many people would not believe. My experiences, as with many other colleagues, range from hilarious to horrific. While we all, male and female, black to white, can share our grievances of being disrespected, there's a subgroup of people who could not possibly circumnavigate encounters with racism and even sexism. A noticeable chunk of our lives would be omitted.

******

I remember when Viagra hit the market. It was the little blue pill that nearly every man wanted but no man wanted anyone to know that he had it. Viagra was a miracle medicine discovered by accident. It was originally manufactured to treat hypertension and angina. Turns out it was more effective at turning "Mickey Mouse" into "Mighty Mouse." Viagra quickly became an enormous success (wink emoji). This was so much so that counterfeiters thought it was a good idea to manufacture a subtherapeutic version of the little blue diamond on the black market. It was even shipped in an official looking Pfizer bottle. It isn't certain how much revenue the company lost over counterfeiting. But fake prescription medications sold online in general became a widespread problem overall costing companies potentially billions of dollars. The worst and often lingering consequence of the malfeasance are the people who bought the hype. Whether consumers were searching for a more cost-effective product, too embarrassed to use a legitimate local pharmacy or had some other motive, they all played the fool. People searched alternative foreign markets to buy something that was domestically tested and proven effective, and available right around the corner.

The belief that a packaged product that looks like the real deal is genuine, audited by only the naked eye is just naïve or better yet, willful ignorance. All the counterfeiters have to do is sell a convincing lie. Then people will buy it. Everyone has a need to *believe, buy and benefit.*

We'll believe and buy just about anything if it benefits us. This is especially true when we adopt false information. And if what is believed albeit untrue, is convincing enough, it creates a domino effect of repercussions. Take the issue here with counterfeit medication. Just because an alternative marketplace advertises a drug that claims to be identical to the real drug it does not make that drug the real thing. You can only get the real thing from the real manufacturers. There's only one true product (in the case of Viagra) distributed through legal channels, sold at legal retailers. But felonious ads that infiltrate the lines of mass communication are believable. As consumers by nature, we constantly have a need to be bought. So, we buy it. Successful sellers know that people deep down have a need to believe, be bought and benefit. We want to believe in something, some person or idea. And absent of factual information, we'll compromise common sense, health, morality and law to do so. This belief in counterfeit information or counterfeit product remains, until we consider the facts. Otherwise, the deceitful seller of lies makes a fortune while the consumer of lies suffers the repercussions. There's always a price to pay for buying into falsehoods.

******

Similarly, is the misinformation pertaining to covid-19 vaccines. I do not have the energy to argue against the illegitimacies here. But I will say that falsehoods about treatments and prevention are rampant. Apparently, everyone in every neighborhood and on social media has a Ph.D. in Virology and Immunology. It is insane that falsehoods in the United States can be more accessible or rather more acceptable than facts. But then I remembered that I was born and raised in a country that in part, historically relied on falsehoods that still plague us today. A demographic of sellers and willing buyers benefited from ridiculous counterfeit ideals. Subsequently, there's always a consequence for believing and buying the bull.

******

Before graduating from Xavier University of Louisiana in 2003, as a part of our exit check off list from the HBCU ecosystem, we were counseled by a couple of administrators who lovingly cautioned us about the real world we were about to face. We had been living under the comfort and care of an HBCU umbrella where we mattered, where we were the majority. Life beyond Xavier University couldn't be more different.

While we were heavily recruited from XULA in the 90s and early 2000s, where we landed was likely to be in places where we were not seen or loved nearly as much. Our existence only mattered so much as it was unavoidable, like at a pharmacy counter or other professional settings. For many African American graduates, after exiting our ecosystem we would likely attend gatherings where we were the only Black people in attendance somewhere in the suburbs to inevitably be questioned by a presumptuous young white male pretending to have never met educated Black people before:

"What do you do for a living?" They might say. Or,

"So, where's Xavier?"

We'd then witness an expression of cluelessness and ultimately a surprised response as my husband explained what an HBCU is.

The Black college grad back then might meet new white colleagues who make excuses as to why they can't shake our hand as both my husband and I experienced. Black college graduates with new money are likely to encounter a white home owner young or old who may be far more comfortable with selling us their home than to have us live next to their home. I never quite determined if we were too young, too black or both. Consequently, we chose to embrace those who embraced us, whatever race.

We also chose to appease on occasion by informing older white neighbors what we did for a living preemptively in an attempt to bypass their curiosity or rather their suspicion. I'm not kidding. We'd do it when asked (and we were asked a lot) or if they didn't. Like we had been trained in white suburbia. Whites asking Blacks, especially the young ones, in upper middle-class neighborhoods '*What do you do for a living?*' outright or roundabout was and sometimes is still a thing (like my lawn guy, the termite bond guy, and one of my son's friends, all white). I blamed their ignorance on not having lived around us and gathering their Black knowledge from how they were raised, blatant omission of our history in school curriculum, mainstream media, local news, and church.

******

All annoyances of the real world aside, for the longest time my MOA was to appease and live peaceably much like I do when filling in shifts for other pharmacists. I'm the visitor. Even in a country I was born and raised in—I'm a visitor. That's biblical; the *peace* part (Rom 12:18). Learn more. Mouth off less. All with a whipped cream topping of *appease and succeed*. That was me. Early in my career, a friend from back home, Sharon, who I attended Xavier with, checked me about my passive attitude one time. She told me I was making excuses for them. She was right.

Then somewhere down the line between retrieving a voicemail while working in Gwinnett County, Georgia, where a woman felt so comfortable with referring to one of my techs as a "nigger," an elderly white male at the same location refusing to allow a Somalian American technician to fill his prescription because he believed he looked like a terrorist, Treyvon Martin being shot through the heart by a wanna-be cop who got away with it, and watching "CBS This Morning" on May 26, of 2020, airing the most horrific modern-day lynching of George Floyd, did I come to terms with how a hateful part of American society sees us.

******

Late one night I was stopped by a state trooper in Effingham County, GA with my toddler daughter in the back seat. We were headed to Little Rock, AR to celebrate our birthdays with my two older sisters, Tracy and Rachelle, who were born in the same month as us. I decided to leave in the wee hours of the night to avoid heavy traffic *and* I thought my daughter would sleep for most of the trip if I left extra early. She was wide awake. I was driving this luxury SUV with a HEMI brand new at the time. Mind you, I'm driving within the speed limit of 70mph on the interstate. All the while I can not only see the state trooper driving in the same direction, but also at least 6 other vehicles zoom right past me. They had to be traveling at least 80 mph. I can see the officer. I think I'm in the safety zone knowing he's about to get one tonight. Turns out he got me. This guy turns his headlights off and drives within a few feet of my SUV as if I don't see him.

"You have got to be kidding me. Who does that?" I whispered annoyingly trying not to alarm my daughter.

I checked on my daughter through the rearview hoping she was asleep. She wasn't. She was observing her surroundings and sucking her thumb as usual. The officer finally turned on his lights and siren. So, I pulled over. I frowned, looking pissed off up to the point he appeared at my door. He was a slender white male about 6ft. tall. He asked for my license and registration. I gave it to him all with a fake smile. He asked where I was headed. I told him. He said,

"This is a real nice vehicle. What is it?"

You just ran my plate asshole you know what it is, I was thinking.

With that fake smile of mine I told him what he already knew.

"Boy it smells good in there. What kind of coffee is that?"

I told him. It was hazelnut flavored. I bought it at a gas station where I filled up enroute before turning onto the interstate. Checking my rearview mirror again I see my daughter looking at him still sucking her thumb unamused but generally aware of what was happening. The officer doesn't look directly at my daughter, but I know he's aware of her in the back seat. This guy goes on to tell me why I was the chosen one and not the speed demons.

"You touched the median a few times while driving."

I glared at him in disbelief. He didn't even make eye contact when telling me this bull. It's not that I didn't do it. It's that I did it while peeking at him in my rearview because he was tailgating me with his headlights off in the dark! I didn't argue. I braced for what I thought was a ticket he was writing. For the life of me, I cannot remember if I used the '*I'm worthy to be driving this vehicle at this hour in this town*' excuse. By that I of course mean telling him I was Dr. So-and-so and what I did for a living as I would do with my nosey white neighbors.

While looking at my license he had to have noticed the expiration date. It was October. At that moment I knew a ticket was imminent. But then it dawned on me that my birthdate hadn't passed. For a moment, I found myself justifying this unreasonable stop no more than 15 minutes enroute to my 14-hour destination. Appeasement. Excuses. One can consider it a mode of survival or a sorry mechanism of action where I constantly apologized for my existence or success. He was satisfied. He gave me back my ID and registration. No ticket. The irony of it all-that at first glance, in a pricey vehicle I was considered a threat by someone who was a threat to me. I don't know if I was too young to be driving that vehicle, too black or both.

I do not condone anyone disrespecting an officer of the law. You will not win. It's best to keep your composure. Do as you are told and nothing more. But if you don't comprehend the ridiculousness of being tailgated in the middle of the night and pulled over while driving within the speed limit just to find out you're being stopped because of an action provoked by law enforcement who should otherwise be protecting you, you are thereby practicing willful ignorance.

******

There is a portion of white society who view Black and any other minority group of any other skin color not *white (or pink)* as *otherness*. It's the selling point for racism, the counterfeit product. It's still the bull that's bought to benefit them. That demographic therefore has been conditioned to hate *otherness*, thus many of them believing in their superiority over *otherness*. Thereby also believing that people not white need to *prove themselves* to those racists. Some Blacks, like myself, fell in line. At least I used to. Possibly even worse is that a noticeable portion of other people of color bought the same bull. Some are conditioned to hate Blacks.

No one wants to be viewed as less than. So, if a dominant group of people views *otherness* as less than and has the means to treat *otherness* as less than, and the known target of that view is Black, well then who would want to be Black? In general, other minority groups are conditioned to believe it's better to be anything but Black. Even while mimicking our blackness. Someone (white) a very long time ago told a very good lie and for so long people bought it as truth, even non-whites.

I'll never forget my husband, Ron, telling me one evening after work about one of his Asian colleagues who, by the way, credited my hubby for teaching him how to dress to impress (à la XU!). He told my husband that he went to see a movie in Atlanta. He jokingly told Ron that he'd observed how there were a lot of "colored people" at the theater. I looked at Ron stupefied. He returned the same look with a sarcastically confused grin. We both laughed at his colleague's contempt. First of all, it's ATLANTA! Second of all,

"WTF?!"

What was worse was that Ron didn't use the opportunity as a teachable moment. No crash course on what the phrase means, how the "colored" water fountain was for the both of them, no lesson on what Jim Crow was, and what his grandson, James Crow, Esq. is. Nothing. So as far as we know to this day, this yellow 1st gen American doesn't know that he's "colored." I suspect many more 1st and 2nd gen Asian Americans do not know as well.

******

They sold the lie. We bought it as truth. So, the lie became a contagion in America with no cure to this day. It is an ideology intricately woven into the fabric of a country that promises liberty while injecting hate. It is injected physically and psychologically, having damaged us psychologically and spiritually. I've lost count of the number of encounters I've had with whites and non-whites presumably with this counterfeit ideology in the back of their minds as their words and actions speak to their prejudices about race.

At this point I am well aware that these encounters have no end in this realm. Because someone told one heck of a good lie. People believed it, bought it and benefited from it. *How so?* You might ask? Simply put, exclusion. Exclude a group from equity, from representation, from equal rights and equal healthcare, from historical importance, and the opposing group benefits from counterfeit ideology. Like fake medications that get passed off as the real thing, this counterfeit idea, marketed as an inferior race that is beneath a superior race, is passed off as if it too is real. The idea has been marketed for so long that it lingers as a point of reference to see and treat people differently because of skin color. It's embedded in our culture so much so, that it affects everyone of us, whether we're beneficiaries or victimized by the lie.

Because incidents involving race are interwoven into my personal and professional life by default, I've found that while I have very little desire to make race the climax in this small body of work, it is totally unavoidable. Furthermore, it has become exhausting to continue pacifying white society and the willfully ignorant in effort to make them feel comfortable. There is no lack of love for white Americans on my part. I don't have the capacity to hate other human beings at this stage in life. I say this while still experiencing blatant and nuanced discrimination. That said, I'd be guilty of an intentional omission if I didn't acknowledge the love I've received throughout my life from various whites, particularly my teachers while growing up. I also appreciate the those that taught me a thing or two along the professional trail.

I thank God that all white people don't think alike. Truthfully. That has been a part of my *'What are you thankful for?'* prayer at the Thanksgiving table for years. I truly thank God for all white people *not* thinking alike. Otherwise, we (minorities, the *others*) would be in a lot of trouble. But just as I am fatigued with explaining and validating my thoughts and experiences as I've resolved to do here, I am also grateful to God that I and other descendants who have lived in this country for so many generations, have survived and many have thrived in spite of hatred and hindrances experienced by each of those generations. I am fatigued after what happened to Floyd. My son and daughter witnessed a modern-day lynching in 2020! Did you have a conversation with your children at the dinner table about what they saw on social media? My husband and I did. It traumatized them. Did your son have a panic attack after being stopped by the police at night with no parents around to protect him? Mine did. Both my children have had encounters with racism before either of them turned 10! Just like their parents! Just like their grandparents and their great grandparents! Yet we are always expected to let it go. To paraphrase Gordon P. Robertson of *The 700 Club*, who commented on the matter,

How many times are people supposed to keep forgiving for the same offenses?

Racist offenders expect forgiveness but they seem never to expect to change. They offer settlements, an orchestrated apology, conviction expungement, denial and even lies. They do not offer recompense. They do not offer reconciliation. They do not offer repentance. No one wants your apology. We want you to change.

Even as I succeed, I have enough sense to understand the impact of this country's past. My success or any other minority's success does not erase racism. It is futile for anyone to continue to deny the existence of racism in America. Even though people like Tim Scott and Nikki Haley would have us believe otherwise. As a reminder to them and for anyone else who denies the reality of racism and the overwhelming impact that it continues to bleed, including paving the way for white privilege, without prejudice, please refer to the international coverage of what happened at the United States Capitol on January 6, 2021, 12:53pm-4:00pm est.

10

It's All in Your Mind
(Placebo Effect)

No patient wants to be told by a practitioner that their
symptoms are imagined. They'd much rather hear that they
have a stomach bug, food sensitivity or extemporaneous
diaphorea (which doesn't exist by the way). Tell them
anything except they are not sick. So from time to time a PCP
or urgent care practitioner may prescribe medicine to an
otherwise healthy pop-up patient. Nothing habit forming. Just
a "remedy" to "cure" their "illness." What might they
prescribe? Sedatives, like Trazodone, to take at night. Or
Hydroxyzine to calm a nervous itch. Sometimes Zyprexa is
prescribed to shut their busy brains off, and induce sleep. If
they're not awake, then they're not worrying. But wouldn't
that make worrying a sickness? People can actually worry
themselves sick. Tests will prove it. There really is no
physical ailment as far as the practitioner can see but a self-
generated thought could perpetuate itself into phantom
symptoms that are felt by the patient. They think it therefore

they believe it. For example, you complain to a nurse practitioner that your feet are burning. He tells you to stand and walk. You stand and walk just fine. They don't feel hot when he touches them. No test can prove a foot burn. Plus, he sees no flame coming from your feet. Therefore, your feet cannot be burning. But you will not leave that office without a remedy for that foot burn. The nurse practitioner leaves, then comes back with a 'scription written for magic white pills.

"Here ya go. These will make it better."

The nurse gives a warm grin and touches your shoulder in reassurance.

"Thank you, doc." You leave satisfied.

Why stroke what's perceived to be phantom symptoms with a smile and no good drugs? Because no one wants to hear that "it's all in your mind." Because practitioners aren't taught how to treat what they don't see or feel. To them, it's all up here (point to your temple).

But what if the burning feet were real and actually symptomatic of uncontrolled diabetes? What if the neglect for a full examination, including blood tests, eventually led to other symptoms including acute kidney failure? What if that patient's entire body shut down from medical neglect? What was perceived to be one's imagination has manifested into a life altering disability. This is what life was like for minority pharmacists early in my career, more assuredly, minorities in professional environments in general.

******

My second internship was also in Memphis, TN in 2001. It was my first employment with W Pharmacy. I wasn't quite ready for my prospective career. Ok, I wasn't ready at all. I had no mentor, no cs and no money. Neither did I have my own car to get around. But I did have family. Thank God for my family.

The previous summer while working my first internship in nearby Madison County, I drove Charles Jr.'s white 1992 Toyota Corolla that had a big dent in the hood. Charles is my oldest brother. He lived in a suburb of Memphis and was moving up in the world. He worked as a financial analyst for a healthcare conglomerate in the city and did taxes on the side. He loved money, made money but hated to spend money. He didn't live like his clients or peers who wore their money on their sleeves. He once splurged on a red Miata, a coup of modest means. But in true frugal fashion, he held on to the first vehicle he ever purchased. It was a green 1992 Chevy pickup truck. He clung to it and that Corolla from yesteryear he bought back in the day for his first wife. They were kind enough to allow me to drive it for the summer. Oh yeah, I lived with them that summer, too. Like I said, thank God for family.

That Rolla was an A to B, B to A kind of ride by this time. But I had to be careful trying to attempt a B to C destination like driving to my parents' house from work on a Friday. They lived in the next state. But because my parents lived nowhere near the interstate, I had to drive through Northwest Mississippi which meant that I had to drive down Highway 61. This was not a big deal except that the hood of the Rolla was kept shut with a thick rubber towing band that had metal hooks on both ends. It was attached from the bent hood to the fender. When accelerating above 50 mph like one would do on Hwy 61, the bottom hook would lose its grip and the hood would fly open. Driving blind I had to pull over, close the dented hood and re-hook the rubber band to the fender. It happened at least 5 times during what should've been a one hour and forty-five-minute trip home. It took me about two-hours and fifteen minutes under the circumstances.

I upgraded the summer of 2001 to one of my parents' cars. A Chrysler Concorde. It was a 1996 model, charcoal gray with a crack, mid-view, clear across the windshield. Looking at it, you just knew it was one jetted highway rock away from collapsing. I drove on a prayer everyday with the hope that crack did not give-way.

I met my soon-to-be supervisor with W Pharmacy in that Chrysler at a pharmacy location in a questionable part of town. We met there for a formal interview for that summer's internship. I knew the company needed to maintain prospective hires as the turnover was so high for pharmacists. So I didn't worry about the interview. Plus, I'd been prepped exhaustively during a previous summer internship at UAMS in Little Rock, AR for job interviews as if I was graduating the next month. It was a tough program but very beneficial. I was well prepared afterwards on how to get my foot in the door. Back then, interns were heavily recruited for this particular company. I knew the internship was in the bag.

What did concern me was where the heck I was. I'd visited Memphis plenty of times but had never been to that part of town. The parking lot was unkept. Trash was laying right outside of a huge green garbage bin. Trash was tossed in the street and parking spaces. I remember what looked like dilapidated apartments. Some windows and doors boarded up. Some with bars. It was early in the day. Too early for neighborhood drama. Then I saw two kids, probably pre-teens, go inside the same pharmacy. Otherwise, I did not see very many people around. But I made it a point to look around for other people while sitting in my parents' car in the parking lot as I appeared to be isolated. The location gave me a bad feeling. I just knew it wasn't the place to linger, day or night. Regretfully, I got there about 15 minutes ahead of the district supervisor.

After checking my surroundings for the fourth time, I saw one of those two kids dart outside of the pharmacy with a hand basket. Then I saw the store manager, an overweight black guy in a gray vest, run after him. The kid was agile. He zigzagged through the parking lot like he was on skates. The manager zagged and zigged but not nearly as fluid. Then the elusive thief ran to the back of the big green garbage bin and put the basket on the ground. While keeping his eye on the gray vested "cop" he managed to place the stolen goods in one of the discarded plastic bags I regarded as trash on the side of the big green bin. As I could not believe what was happening right in front of me while waiting for my future boss to arrive, I noticed with attentive eyes what the kid was putting in the bag. It was a half-gallon of milk and a carton of eggs. Still on the lookout he quickly tied the plastic bag and set his feet in gear to take off. The manager was anticipating him to reemerge, looking from left to right but clearly hoping from his heavy breathing to not have to run full speed anymore. Even so, he was eager to catch the perp for snatching less than $10 worth of goods. The boy then took off like a track star in a 400. Game over. The feat was quite impressive and disheartening at the same time. What child goes to a corner store to steal milk and eggs? I surmised the kind of kid whose mother told him to do it.

My soon-to-be district supervisor arrived, parking right beside my car. I'll refer to him as "Jon." Upon getting out to meet him I noticed he was distracted by the crack in the windshield of my parents' car. I redirect his attention by recounting the misadventure that occurred right before he got there. Surely that was much more concerning. A better question was why he had chosen such a crappy location as a first impression for an interview.

The interns were courted hard by recruiting supervisors. I was one of about twenty that summer in the Memphis area. The district was split into two; Memphis East and Memphis West. My supervisor was my brother's age. He was a confident, slightly arrogant, suit-wearing chubby white guy who smiled a lot and was easy to talk to. As I mentioned, prospective pharmacists were courted hard. We were fed and housed on the company's dime and taken to a semi-professional baseball game at some point during the summer. Our supervisor from time to time would check in with us or swipe us away from our work sites for half a day. He'd take a few interns at a time from their respective locations to show them around town to see the chain's numerous pharmacy sites. He touted the stability of the company and ongoing growth, how they were better than the competition. After the touting, he taunted the competitors by bringing us right inside of their pharmacies to prove how inferior they were. I thought it was bold and hilarious at the time. We stepped inside "K Pharmacy" one time and planted ourselves in one of the OTC aisles. Our summer supervisor began his taunting,

"Look at how they do that... At our pharmacy we do this."
He goes on,

"Look at how they're set up, it's all wrong. We do much
better. That's why we are better," he bragged.

"Hi Jon! How's it going today?" The pharmacist on duty
called him by name. He heard every word.

"Hi, how ya doin'?! I'm just showing them around," Jon said,
grinning the whole time.

I could just imagine Pharmacist So-and-So at K Pharmacy
calling my supervisor all kinds of so-and-so's to himself.
What a jerk.

I started the internship a week later than everyone else
because my parents' Chrysler needed some repairs. I was
hoping that meant the windshield was being replaced. It
didn't. Having been informed about my temporary
transportation deficiency, my boss assigned me to a
pharmacy near the dorms at the University of Memphis
where all of the interns were lodging. I wasn't sure if he
thought I was going to catch the bus or walk to work that first
week, but I refused to do either until my parents' car was
fixed. Maybe I was a snob for doing that. But I saw it as a
safety precaution back then. In hindsight it was 80% the
former, 20% the latter.

The pharmacy where I worked was located in a busy part of
the city. Maybe Park Street, South Parkway, or something.
On second thought, I believe South Parkway is where I blew
a tire on the Corolla the previous summer. Anyway, it was a
24-hour location, an all-Black staff and a pharmacy manager

who openly admitted that he never paid his taxes.

"They'll have to take me to jail! Hoohoo, Ah-heeheehee!"

He had the most ridiculous laugh. In no way did it match his face or speech. He was a tall fair-skinned guy with a noticeable birthmark on his face, very poised and down to business, until he cracked himself up, laughing at his own banter. Then he became a country-Bama clown. That infectious laugh made it impossible not to laugh along with him.

I pissed him off one day during a hectic shift. I thought he told me to get a prescription from another pharmacy. I translated that verbiage to mean that he wanted me to get a "copy" from the other pharmacy. That means to call another pharmacy and request that the pharmacist go on a patient's profile to get prescribing information for an existing prescription for a patient. That prescription is transcribed verbally from their system to us with the remaining refills so that we can fill the prescription at our location. A few minutes later this man comes over to me and asks,

"Did you transfer the prescription?"

"They said they didn't have the prescription," I responded a little confused.

He snatches the company prescription paper out of my hand that he had given to me, rolled his eyes and said,

"I'll do it myself," and he walked away.

So, of course by his rude response I figured out he wanted me to give the other pharmacy the drug written on the pad which was a refill on the patient's profile at our location so that they could fill it instead. I didn't realize. Oh well.

He must've felt bad about it later or was made to feel bad by one of the technicians. We happened to leave for our break at the same time and he invited me to lunch after apologizing. I declined lunch. Then I smiled and told him that everything was fine, that I had to learn. He smiled back. It was a genuine exchange. I was glad he apologized. But from then on, I decided that certainty was better than assumptions. So, when in doubt, ask. I asked a lot. A whole lot. Because I realized I didn't know shit. Academic knowledge is futile without practical experience. Internships were valuable and boy did I bug the hell out of the staff that summer, and the following year too, while working during school. I saw the annoyance at times but I did not care. I had to learn. They got theirs. I needed to get mine—work experience that is.

That summer in Memphis proved to be quite interesting as it turned out. On one of the outings with the supervisor, we visited what I thought was a random location. That is until we saw there were two minority female pharmacists. I'm sure he wanted us to see the diversity within the family of the #1 pharmacy chain. He was chatting away while there.

The manager was a Black woman who appeared to be about 50 years old with a lot of gray hair. I mean what I thought was a lot of streaks of gray hair for her age. She looked stressed to a point of concern. I recall him touching her shoulder and asking if she was doing better. She nodded looking toward the floor as if something serious had occurred. He removed his hand and moved on to discussing business as usual. The other pharmacist there was an Indian young lady (a real Indian not the misnomer), no more than 30. She talks to the boss as if resuming some conversation that had begun from another day. He gave her that warm grin, reassuring her that everything would be fine and glided on out of there. As we were leaving in the company car, Jon informed me and the other interns that the Indian pharmacist accused a white male pharmacist of "being prejudice" against her.

"It's all in her mind," he said with that familiar grin while backing out of the parking lot.

******

The interns met with a representative from the company's brokerage firm, which was Merryl Lynch at the time. They served us lunch and we had a Q&A afterwards. It was great—the food I mean. The rep talked about what ML did for the company, their employees, how we were going to make a lot of money soon and that we should give it to them. I can safely assume back then that most, if not all of us youngsters, in year one or two of pharmacy school were on the same page when I say that we didn't give a rat's ass about investing and had no clue as to what ol' boy in the overpriced suit was talking about. But the grub and the time away from our busy sites were appreciated. Plus, the interns liked seeing each other and swapping stories from the apothecary.

There was one older Black gentleman I met at the meeting. He was a tall, brown-skinned guy, with 2-inch-high black hair and a low fade. A handsome man especially with his glasses on. He looked at least 4 years older than me. I'll call him "Randy." I could tell he was big on impressions. His clothes were dry cleaner pressed. He wore a business blue long sleeve button down shirt and gray slacks that raised to a respectable height while he was seated, revealing black socks and shiny black tied dress shoes. I remember him vividly because he was only one of three Black men in the program that summer. You couldn't help but smile at this handsome brown-skin dude. But he wasn't in a smiling mood. After sharing our experiences so far, he informed me that he wasn't happy with the location he was assigned to. I asked why.

"It's in a bad location. On 3rd Street," he informed me.

I knew the street well. It's a very long road where I knew of seeing at least two of the chain's pharmacies. Third Street is that road we travel down to get to any of our relatives' homes or to get to downtown when driving into Memphis from Arkansas. It has never been a site for sore eyes. It was just sore...like a bad scab.... that never healed...that got gangrene. You want someone to cut it off and get rid of it but they can't because it's necessary for travel and commerce. We only stopped along 3rd Street out of convenience to fill up on gas when visiting.

Randy wanted to be reassigned but remained there for the summer. He felt blindsided by the placement. He first assumed that it was a mentorship sequester. But when he asked the pharmacy manager who was also a Black male if he requested to have a Black male at his location, the manager told him,

"No, they just keep sending me Black male interns."

He didn't request anybody. Randy was really unnerved by the matter. He went on telling me,

"The white females in the programs were in the suburbs and near the new mall. They got the better locations"

I wanted to contest because I knew of at least one white young lady working at this non-drive thru parcel location that happened to be the #2 location in the country for that pharmacy chain at the time. They averaged 1100 prescriptions a day our supervisor told us. That place had to be a super hell hole. I remembered the pictures of the pharmacists on the wall just outside of that pharmacy. There were a lot of them, men and women, and that they were almost all white. No Blacks. But I did find out he was right about most of the white female interns being placed in the burbs. But I was certain that a couple of Black females were assigned to good locations as well. At least I knew they didn't complain, not to me when I asked them. I also asked one of the other two Black male interns in the program where he was assigned. Take a wild guess where. He's at the other 3rd Street location. He confessed that it was really bad there, people stealing, the cops on site for robberies or theft, and rude customers. It sounded worse than the first 3rd Street pharmacy. But he wasn't the type to complain.

Then it hit me. The location by the dilapidated homes and theft where I was interviewed....my boss had intended to assign me there. Initially, I believed the only reason it didn't happen is because of the theft I'd witnessed. Rather, it was more than likely because of my parents' Chrysler with the cracked windshield that needed maintenance. I couldn't give Jon a timeline for the repair. So, he possibly switched my assigned pharmacy only because that crappy location was too far to walk to or to take the bus from the dorm I lived in for the summer. Was it possible Jon was assigning interns by racial preference? Did he think he was avoiding a problem by placing the Black male interns with Black male pharmacy managers? Did he purposely place white female interns in the burbs under white managers? Why would you meet a new intern in the worst part of town for an interview? Because I was Black? I couldn't prove any of the aforementioned but the pieces sure did fall into place.

Then one day Jon came for a one-on-one visit to my site to check in with me. We met in the manager's office. He must've gathered the uninterested vibe of the interns at the ML meeting. He began talking up the company 401k, stocks and stock options and asked if I understood what either was. I admitted I didn't.

"That's ok. I'll show you," he said.

He took a sheet of paper from the inkjet printer and gave me a not-so-elementary explanation of purchasing shares and exercising options. Options were offered by the company based on the 1000th new location. Whether or not you were offered options and how many depended on when you were hired. You exercised those options when you became vested. In my case it was Options 3000. I was given 100 options, I think. Or maybe it was 300. Then Options 4000 rolled around after I graduated. Long story short, the options were good if you knew how and when to exercise them. The stock was also good. The 401k was fantastic.

So, there he was, my boss the informative jerk, teaching me

about stock options and passive income in dividends. I began to second guess the claims Randy made and even my own observations while in the program since the interview. I second guessed the accusation made by the Indian pharmacist he blew off and the distressed female pharmacy manager who looked like she needed a transfer if not a sabbatical.

I made an effort to probe into Jon's personal life. He clearly wasn't a monolithic employee. I was suddenly interested in the life of a person four levels above my pay grade. I asked him questions about himself, his career and where he went to pharmacy school. I don't remember where he went to pharmacy school. I do remember what he said about himself. He admired himself a lot. He impressed himself as a student. He mentioned how during clinicals he would bs about patient profiles by holding a blank sheet of paper in his hand, giving made up stats to professors about patients' disease states and prognoses. He made up pharmacotherapies and would adjust the dosages or discontinue meds that he knew all about from class and working in pharmacies for years. His intention back in school was to be exactly what he was, a pharmacy supervisor, and a corporate position was next. He believed his way of thinking was necessary for the types of jobs he aspired to. He talked about his interview for his current position. It was all about the ability to communicate exceptionally well from what he told me. Jon had the gift of gab. There was no real substance, no real empathy. He used skills of persuasion and focused on results. That was corporate competence. The awareness of operational outcomes along with the ability to prioritize profit over environment was the game. He worked for the corporation, not the employees.

The employees were means to an end, like commodities running a money machine. His job was to pull in the commodity. Plug them into the machine so they can produce money. Then replace the commodities when they collapse. The intricacies of why they're collapsing is not his concern. Replacing them is. That's why the internships were so important. The goal is to keep the money machine running.

Then there was his home life. His wife did not work. He didn't want her to. Her duties were him, the house and their kids. That's the way he wanted it. He said it. He didn't mention what his wife wanted. I made the comment that I didn't think I could (or would) wing it the way he did in school when it came to patient profiles during clinicals. After all, they're not scenarios. They're real-life cases, real health problems of real-life people. His response was,

"Oh, then you couldn't do this [job] then." He said it with that arrogant grin. *What a jerk.*

My overall impression of Jon was mixed. The same charismatic guy that introduced me to entry level investing is the same jerk that appeared to believe racial and gender discrimination was a myth. Or at least he treated it that way. The fact that he ignored racial disparities within a local unit that he not only may have propagated but perpetuated was but a portion of a bigger problem exacerbated by corporate-level executives.

The professional culture of ignoring "burning feet" or merely treating issues perceived by upper-level management as phantom ideas with placebo was common practice for decades. Discrimination against race and gender were embedded in the overall corporate culture. Those who practice willful ignorance gladly benefit from it and simply look the other way. Then there are those who are fully aware that it exists but because they have a place within the culture, the fear of losing what they have outweighs the desire to fight against it. It's just easier to assimilate. The practice couldn't possibly change when the person being affected by it is told "it's all in your mind." All the while the reported "burning feet" are just the beginning of an eroding organ system within retail pharmacy. The results of which end with understaffing, high turnovers that can no longer be remedied, locations closing, and a once flourishing company being bought out by other big box pharmacies or a private equity firm.

By the way, Jon landed a big promotion at the corporate office a few years later. I'm sure he fit right in.

11

Shake Vigorously Before Pouring

That same thought-provoking summer that I spent as an intern for W Pharmacy in Memphis, Tennessee, I stopped at a Wendy's restaurant near the University of Memphis for dinner after returning from Nashville. I was still lingering mentally on all that I had heard from Randy, the intern, and my own on-boarding experience.

I know that I frown when I'm deep in thought. Surely, I looked like I wanted to be left alone sitting there at Wendy's. But apparently a self-proclaimed evangelical didn't think so. A lady with a Bible in her hand, wearing a white t-shirt, an ankle long yellow skirt and brown flats interrupted me, myself and I. She was proclaiming, per her prophetic vision, that I would receive the very thing I had been asking for recently,

"I just want you to know you're going to receive it! What you've been asking for, God's going to give it to you. He's going to give it to you," and some other stuff she said.

"Yes ma'am. Ok and I thank you," I replied with a warm smile.

I was believing this woman, all wrapped up in the moment of the façade. Until I remembered that I hadn't asked God for a thing. She went about "ministering" to others who were eating and minding their own business. I walked out without finishing my food before she made her way back around to my table to collect the offering. I learned later that she was likely to be one of those foot trafficking false prophets that liked to profit from the word of God. One of them who looked a lot like her came into the pharmacy trying to pocket an OTC cream enroute to using the restroom. The senior technician caught her and snatched the cream out of her hand. The woman then followed the tech to the pharmacy and went into Christian shaming mode by giving an impromptu sermon on agape love. The tech wasn't hearing it,

"Who are you to preach to me about agape love? I know what agape love is." the tech responded, rolling her eyes at her.

"She was trying to steal this," she told us slamming the cream on the counter.

I suppose fearing further embarrassment, all the *evilgelical* could do was find her face and leave.

When I hopped in the car to leave the Wendy's parking lot, turns out I couldn't go anywhere. The car wouldn't start.

You have got to be kidding me, I said to myself, I and me.

I tried three more times and then stopped as I seemed to be "flooding" the car. I didn't really know what that meant. I did know everybody said it in the 90s when they tried starting an old car multiple times and the car won't start.

"I can't believe this!" I grunted.

I then noticed steam coming from the hood. So, I popped it open. Now I had seen this similar scene before when I was a little kid where my mom made the error of opening the cap while there was still steam coming from the antifreeze aqueduct. It spewed antifreeze and it got all over her shirt. But this was Memphis after dawn. I was alone and could think of worse things happening to me. So, I removed the top slowly. The manager came out. She fussed at me for taking the top off and asked if I needed help. I told her I would be fine and she went back inside. I wasn't fine. The car wouldn't cool off fast enough. It was getting dark and I was frustrated nearly to tears. Oh, and with no cell phone. It was the summer of 2001. I got my first cell phone the following winter. Yeah, about 6 months too late. I found a nearby payphone and called my aunt and uncle, who lived in the city. Crying and complaining about the car, I sobbed,

"Uncle Russell, the car is smoking and overheated! And it won't start and I'm at Wendy's and....!"

My uncle has this President Barak Obama kind of demeanor. He doesn't react, doesn't get aroused by emotional people. He's unmoved. In fact, in all my years of knowing him I've never heard him raise his voice. Now his wife, my mom's sister, Aunt "Lizzy"? She's the polar opposite. A pistol....as in she once pulled out a pistol in a neighborhood drive-by threatening two teenagers after they intentionally scared her baby sister outside of her house who was living with her at the time. Aunt Lizzy deserves her own chapter.

I'm pretty sure uncle Russell was eating at the dinner table while I was talking to him hysterically through my snotty tears. All I could hear in between my cry was,

"Mmmhmm, Mmmhmm,"

And what I'm sure was closed mouthed chewing. Uncle Russell was a licensed mechanic. Knowing I had nothing I needed, he told me to get a big cup from the Wendy's. Fill it with ice water and pour it in the aqueduct. That would get me back to the dorm. Then call my dad from there. The Chrysler had to be operated on yet again. Some kind of tube in the car had a big hole in it. I had just come from Nashville where I spent a week working as a part of my internship. Then drove back to Memphis on I 40 West. I was driving 3 hours one way at 80mph in a car with a big fat hole in a tube that looked really important! That car had way more problems than I was aware of. I don't know if my parents were protecting me by not telling me or simply letting me drive off and hoping for the best. The cracked windshield was the least of that car's issues.

My dad replaced that destroyed tube in a day's shift. I don't know how I got to work. I must have hitched a ride that morning. My dad and my mom showed up at my job. I was so happy to see them. Later, at Charles Jr.'s house, I told them everything that had happened including my new concern about the optics of the program with the assigned stores designated by my boss. That internship was a big opportunity. I wanted to believe in what I thought was positive, not what might appear negative. Maybe I was overthinking it.

******

I developed summer friendships with some other interns and one white guy who you would've thought surfed right out of the West Coast. He had long curly hair. A loose t-shirt and palm tree printed shorts or khaki's above the knee were his main attire. We hung out a bit here and there on campus.

I was invited to go with a group of other female interns to a club called *Denim n Diamonds*, one night. He happened to come by while I was getting ready.

"Whatcha up to?"

"I got invited to a club with some of the girls."

I chose to go out in my '*I ain't never been to a club. I hope I got this right*' outfit. I didn't get it right. Too much of my body was not showing. My curly headed friend wanted to tag along.

"Hey I can go with..?" I looked at him imagining him in the club with those short shorts on. I smiled, looking up at him while putting on one shoe.

"No, I don't think that would be a good idea inviting someone at the last minute. Plus, I'm not driving."

I made an excuse because I thought it was rude to invite someone else, particularly a male, to hop along in someone else's car with 3 other females who didn't know him. Well apparently, he took offense and wouldn't speak to me the next day in the cafeteria. I didn't mean to make him feel unwelcome. I thought he was being too sensitive. He didn't spend any more time with me after that.

******

A few days later I was invited to dinner at a Mexican restaurant with a group of white girls all in the same program as me. Or at least I think they all were. I didn't really want Mexican but I was bored and had no idea where my roommate was. Actually, she was probably with her man. The Black girl crew hadn't come by that day so I didn't have any reason not to go. We all piled in one of the girl's black Bronco SUVs. I rode in the back with two or three others while they gossiped but I didn't really listen to their stories about whatever. We got a booth when we got to the restaurant squeezing all of our butts on both sides. Still not really listening to their conversation I noticed Hispanic men who appeared to be Mexican staring at me. I thought it was weird. But I knew why. I also thought it was weird to see Mexicans eating at a Mexican restaurant. (Note to self: since I never consider it weird to see Black folks at a soul food joint, a place I would have much rather gone to eat, then I shouldn't deem the aforementioned weird either.)

While we were looking over the menu of *101 ways to make a taco*, the girl who drove asked while looking at the menu what I was going to order.

"Angie, are you getting the beef or the chicken?"

"Umma get the chicken *chimichainguuuh*," I told her in my countriest vernacular while looking at the menu.

I look up to see one of the Hispanic men still staring as the waitress approaches. I order first:

"I'll have the beef chimichanga."

On the way back to the dorm I happened to tune in to the Bronco convo. The girl driving shared a sexcapade she had with some random guy. Or maybe it was her boyfriend. She freely admitted to the group that the guy gave her mono. I freely took that info back to the dorm to tell my roommate and the Black girl crew.

******

My roommate, Leah, was a year younger than me as most of the interns were. She was a tall, athletic white young lady with long brown hair and very friendly. She was also engaged to be married. We hit it off great. I mistakenly thought she was Black prior to meeting her. When I moved in, her clothes and bedding were there. Her bed had a purple comforter with white and black designs. The bedding was black satin including a black satin pillowcase. It was a satin pillowcase. Go figure. Her wedding was scheduled for later that summer. She never hung out with the white girl crew or anyone else for that matter other than her fiancé or myself. We went speed walking a time or two together. We may have gone to the library and definitely to the cafeteria together. Otherwise, we'd chitchat in the room.

Not long after we got acquainted, I found her in a mood over her fiancé, Greg, and his mother. Greg wouldn't man up and

143

defend her when his mother provoked her to anger. His mother also unfairly used him as a replacement husband, depending on him way too much. She shared quite a bit of her grievances about her family-to-be. So I thought it would be a good idea to get out and go to lunch to get her mind off of her troubles. Only thing is I forgot that I didn't have a car.

"You mind driving us to take you out to eat?" I asked her unashamed.

We went to this deli nearby. All I could think about was the pound of bread I would have to consume. We sat down and looked over the menu. I didn't like the waiter. He was strange. I assure you that I am not a paranoid person. A hypochondriac maybe, but definitely not paranoid. He acted strange. He smiled way too wide as if the expression was forced. And he bent way too low to greet us and to take our order. I did not like how he looked at me. I'm sure my face showed my displeasure. So, I turned to my roommate when he left to get our glasses of water. I wanted to see if she saw what I saw. She was too preoccupied with the menu of *33 ways to make a ham n cheese sandwich*. The waiter returned with the water. We both ordered. I chose roast beef. Again, he's smiling too wide and bending way too hard. First turning her way then swaying to turn my way. It was super weird, super suspicious. It took him a little too long to return with our food for a place that only had a few customers as far as I could see. I bit into my sandwich and began to chew when I damn near choked on black pepper in my throat. I took a big gulp of water.

"*That SOB!*" I said in my head.

"Is there pepper on your sandwich?" I asked my roommate.

"No, I don't taste any."

"There's pepper on my roast beef, way too much pepper!" I looked behind me daring the waiter to come back to the table.

Leah looked at me in a crass *'you're being ridiculous'* kinda way while slightly grinning.

"I don't think he put pepper in your sandwich," she said to me.

How you gonna tell me it doesn't have pepper when I'm choking on the pepper?!

I didn't say that. But my expression did. I looked under the French baguette for the incriminating evidence. Then I looked for the waiter. Nowhere to be found.

"If I wanted black pepper, I would've asked for black pepper. He's trying to choke me!"

I know I sounded nuts and probably looked nuts at the time. But I was pepper poisoned. I don't think we went out to eat again after that. But at least I got her mind off of her fiancé drama for a little bit.

My summer internship experiences taught me a few things. First was the importance of family. Thank God for family. Second, people are individuals first. It's not ok to judge based on generalizations or preconceived ideas. I may meet a million people as a pharmacist. It's important to treat each one, as one. And third, racism isn't going anywhere.

12

The 7 Cs

It is well-known that your college years will offer some of the best (and worst) experiences of your life. Nearly all of those experiences have everything to do with the 7 Cs depending on where you went to college: Co-Ed College Campus, Credit Cards, Church and Cults.

My alma Mata, was unique in that it is not only an HBCU, but also a Catholic-based institution that strongly encourages faith-based living. They don't force Catholicism on students, notwithstanding there was only one house of worship on campus, a chapel where mass is open to all who wish to attend. What I appreciated was that other church recruitment was allowed early in the school year. Representatives from different denominations were invited to set up tables in one of the buildings on campus on a specified day so that students could have the opportunity to learn about and hopefully become active members at a local church. New Orleans was never short of churches. I and my freshman roommate for one semester, Emerald, who became one of my closest friends 'til this day, came with me. We focused on the Baptist tables.

******

Emerald and I were roommates at the beginning of freshman year. We both filled out this compatibility survey the summer prior to the school year. Whoever placed us together was spot on. I called her my light-skinned twin. When my oldest sister, Tracy, met her, she offered to trade me in for Emerald as a sweeter version me. Our only difference other than the obvious was a few inches in height. I was taller. And I'm sure she won't mind me saying that she had curves and I didn't. I was actually nicer than her. Back then I hated making other people feel bad even if I was treated that way. I even used to turn the tv to another channel when people got booed on the Apollo. I hated that. Emerald on the other hand would whip a facial expression that refused to hide her feelings especially if they were negative. If she disapproved of anything or anyone, you knew it before she said a word. And my girl was not known for sparing other people's feelings.

We were on the main campus walking to the cafeteria for lunch one day when one of my classmates, Measure, came out of nowhere and accompanied us on the way to eat lunch. He seemed upset, rambling on about the flunkies on the wall. The wall was the rear exit of the convent, an area students considered sacred as the nuns still reside there. But the flunkies with the Swishers didn't care. Anyway, somewhere in between the rambling, Measure looked back at the flunkies rolling his eyes as we continued to the caf and said,

"They over there laughing at me, calling me Sprite 'cause of what I got on."

Emerald and I simultaneously looked to our right to glance at him. Measure was wearing a yellow Polo short-sleeved shirt tucked neatly into his belted, khaki green shorts. Emerald burst into laughter. I couldn't even hear the rest of what he saying. The girl laughed and laughed all the way to the caf. I bucked my eyes at her to reprimand. She knew what I was thinking, *'he's right there, girl.'* She didn't care. Showing solidarity to my classmate, I told him,

"They have no business being over there in the first place."

I was frowning while looking back at them. I quickly turned around and kept it moving. There was zero interaction with those flunkies on my part. Incidentally, I would be their next victim on another day.

******

We optimistically began our church search. I went one way. Emerald went another. You had to be strategic during campus recruitment of any kind (church, organizations, clubs, credit card reps, etc.) in my opinion. If not, you'll walk up to any eye-catching table thinking you're grounded in your respective faith and values but walk away questioning everything you've been taught about being born again. You might meet a cult leader with other students at his headquarters, aka "the yard" on campus for your first "service." You could naively sign up for a credit card just so you could get a free t-shirt, not realizing you can't possibly pay it off if you max out the $700 limit, then accidently joining the U.S. Armed Forces thinking your signature was just a part of a petition expressing patriotism.

BEWARE OF RECRUITING SEASON.

By the time Emerald and I were done with church shopping, after speaking with the reps and grabbing a hand full of pamphlets and knick knacks to remember them by, one of us called the other from our dorm rooms after we both narrowed down where we would like to attend church the following Sunday. Not by coincidence I believe, we both chose the same church. The representative was the pastor. I thought it was quite cool that the leader of the church thought we were important enough to be there himself to speak with the students. From the info that was provided, it sounded like home. Emerald agreed. We made arrangements to attend. Unlike the mega churches who picked up students by bus, we had the privilege of being chauffeured by a member who was about 10 years or so older than us. To be more accurate and more appropriate, she was more than that. Chrissandra became more like an older sister and one of the coolest members we had a relationship with at the church.

We eventually became very close with her, the pastor and his wife there. We never officially joined the church. But we became active and long-term attendees, nonetheless. We joined the Young Adult Ministry and regularly attended Sunday School and service afterwards. We fit right in. A couple of other friends from campus by our sophomore year made that church their home including my then boyfriend, Ronald, who everyone called Ron, and Sharon, who was from my hometown. Other friends and acquaintances would come through from time to time to visit especially during mid-terms and finals. The pastor, Rev. Thomas and his wife, Sis. Nat, took us in as their own. We learned a lot about the city, our university, and the local New Orleans culture from being attached at the hip to them. We never met a stranger either because of them. Understand, that when you travel with the pastor and wife, you're treated the way they are treated, with love and respect. They were regularly invited to other churches and other member's homes. This was common practice back then, particularly with mid-sized Baptist (and COGIC) churches. It was a welcomed privilege to have the pastor and his wife over for Sunday dinner, especially after a slamming sermon (praise hands emoji). It was a bigger privilege if you were a broke college student to be welcomed by proximity to eat at a member's dinner table.

I cannot emphasize enough the love we received and how kind it was for the pastor and wife to allow us to dine where they dined after Sunday service on occasion. It ranged from eating in someone's home or a restaurant they introduced us to. I had not heard of Piccadilly before then. I'm sure of it. I do know Piggly Wiggly. Not the same thing. I must say, however, the best cuisine you can possibly have in New Orleans was at a church member's dinner table. Red beans and rice were a staple. Who had the best red beans and rice? Everyone had the best red beans and rice. We dined on authentic NO jambalaya, crawfish etouffee and rice, Cajun fish, fried fish, gumbo, chicken made any way you can think of, mashed potatoes, sweet potato/yams, rolls, cornbread, greens and green beans. We ate pecan pie, peach pie, apple pie, and pies I couldn't identify. I learned about a local snack, a delicacy in my opinion, called chicken mold that was eaten with saltine crackers. It was delicious. We visited one home where dessert was offered. Sis. Nat took the liberty of warning us before we laid eyes on it. It was called a Punchbowl cake. It didn't seem like a big deal until it was brought to the table. My eyes had never gazed so wide at so much edible Southern pride assembled as one multi-layered, whipped cream, fruit-filled dessert. This cake was a monster sized cake, at least 6 layers of decadent goodness. Sis. Nat burst into laughter after seeing my reaction.

In general, back then, New Orleans residents were happy to welcome you into their homes, especially to eat; particularly if you were a struggling, hungry college student. Most of us were. Everyone believed they had the best food. They loved to cook and loved offering food to eat. No one had to ask us twice.

******

During Mardi gras at the Zulu parade a group of us from the University stopped by a resident's home enroute to eat. Aside from the group leader, Angela, I don't think anyone knew where we were let alone who's house we were in. We were served the ever-available authentic red beans and rice. It was so authentic, everything was thrown in it; pig sausage, pig ear, pig snout and pig toe. All of it simmered and mixed in a dark, reddish-gray rue. What were we supposed to do? Say thanks but no thanks, ma'am? We followed the leader. Fixed a small plate. Sat on the floor and ate. Ron got the snout (lol emoji). He cleaned his plate. I just looked at him.

"Thank you so much for feeding us," Angela said with such a conservative smile. "We appreciate your hospitality. Everybody?"

"Yes, thank you!" Our group replied as prompted. Then we went on our way.

No such worries when we were under the care of our pastor.

People served Rev. Thomas and Sis. Nat their very best. So, we always ate and were treated with the very best.

******

The Thomases made sure we remembered who we were in Christ when we were in their presence. Needless to say, we were expected to do so when not in their presence as well. It reminded me of my grandparents, great-aunts and uncles after church service constantly reminding me when I came home from college to visit. They'd say, "don't give up" and to "hang in there, baby. We'll be praying for you." I took some of that love and concern for granted. Thinking they were only speaking of the cost of higher learning and hard work. Remembering who we were would later prove to be easy to forget as college students. Somehow the deeper we dove into our studies and campus living, the more our priorities shifted, as we became distracted from our *first love*. If you manage to miraculously get through college without fault or blemish, congratulations! You deserve a round of applause. I didn't so much experiment as I did indulge. I really fooled myself. I wasn't nearly as grounded as I believed I was. All it took was one guy. One.

The ratio of men to women on campus was 1:15. If you were one of those men, you would gladly take advantage. The guys had way too many options. And they exercised them to full capacity. One friend who I'm sure was a dud in high school but changed his whole persona the minute he stepped on the college campus to status *Mack*, called my roommate having a more than friendly conversation. Then 30 minutes later called me to have the same. I can't remember if I embarrassed him then or bust him out later for being a rookie at macking.

As for my future hubby, who I met freshman year, he claimed to be oblivious to young ladies hitting on him in undergrad. He *was* on the shy side. I liked that. I took my shot with the shy guy freshman year. We took speech class together as did 10 other females. On our way back to our dorms or the caf, depending on your post-class destination, I'd see a different grinning female walking back with him. I'm never pressed. So, I waited my turn. Fortunately for me that day he had to carry this huge prop he brought to class, a boombox, back to his dorm. That meant he had to walk slower. That also meant I had more time to flirt. I made him laugh. It must've been genuine. I could see all of his upper white teeth. Plus, his big dark brown eyes danced. They still do these days when he's amused. Ron was the sweetest guy. Way too kind to remind me he was carrying a 20lb radio in one hand a mile back to his dorm room. No reciprocating flirtation. No date. Nothing after that. Didn't even ask me for my digits. I gave him my phone number in class one day after missing a G-Chem assignment. Surely, he'd get the hint. He called. He gave me the info I needed.

Then he politely said with a lack of certainty in his voice, "Okaaaay. See you in class." (eyeroll emoji)

He cannot be that blind, I thought. Yet he said he was. What Ron won't admit is that he was attracted to (and pursued) this tall, light-skinned long, curly-haired classmate. Who, by the way, friend zoned him. I probably should've called and thanked her. Ron eventually swayed my way at the beginning of our sophomore year. Right when I had forgotten all about him, calling him "Donald" when we had lunch together with his friend, Morris, and Emerald.

******

My second semester roommate freshman year, Sharon and I were almost lured by what turned out to be a cult leader. Somehow our curiosity led us into a conversation with an upper classman touting pseudo enlightenment. He even designated one of us in the group as a contact person to keep the engagement going with his new "club." We were to meet somewhere other than his main office (a campus parking lot). We almost fell for it. Someone soon after exposed him and the red flag was raised. He was another false teacher/preacher that spent more time recruiting freshmen men and unsuspecting women ultimately for the sake of having orgies. He got this apartment that year where he invited his congregants to christen it. I think he was successful in the beginning because some first-year students can be quite gullible, especially females. When you're away from home one of the first things you seek is acceptance. You want to be seen, welcomed and loved. Easy targets. One female recruit who didn't return after freshmen year was loved a lot by multiple male members from what I was told.

Our campus was small. So, if you did something salacious in secret, well, unless you did it solo, your secret wasn't a secret for long. If you were known for preferring multiple sex partners at one time, the secret got out. If someone fondled their roommate at night thinking she was asleep, the whole dorm found out. If you told someone you slept with a professor, it was told to everyone in the pharmacy building by the end of the week. If you gave your boyfriend a butt-naked lap dance and your roommate innocently knocked on the door that flew open because it wasn't locked properly possibly revealing the sun and moon to her and a loud-mouth suitemate who happened to be in the vicinity, you better believe it was the talk the campus the next day. All campus scandals are subject to co-ed campus gossip. BEWARE.

******

I don't know if credit card reps ever get paid to bait and catch college students on campus grounds like they used to, but I fault administrators for allowing it. They must've given some donation pursuant to being totally visible in effort to entice broke students to register for their memberships into the *American Debt Society*. How in the world can people who already owe tons of money the day they sign promissory notes, be allowed to sign on to an agreement of interest charges ranging from 15-29% on purchases? It's predatory. We would have needed an entire course in order to digest the reality of what we were signing up for. I didn't get lured as a student, but I definitely had my cyclical bouts with credit card usage as a full-fledge adult. Beware smart people. BEWARE.

On the flip side, credit cards can be one's saving grace. Being six hours away from home made for long trips to my destination. So, a credit card was necessary.

I'm from a small town. No major airport. No train station. No bus station. So even if I flew "home" that would mean flying to Memphis, then a one-and-a-half-hour drive to my actual home in Phillips Co. Arkansas. My very first flight ever, Charles Jr. paid for. Our university did not have a shuttle service for students. Neither did we have an airline kiosk like Tulane University down the street. So, I was grateful to my brother for making the flight arrangements. He flew a lot for

his job back then on his company's dime and extended the
courtesy of using frequent flyer miles as an alternative to a
long bus ride.

I scheduled a shuttle pick up provided by the airport shuttle
service that a lot of students used. It was $15 or $20 back
then. Way too much for a service that would pick us up
before heading to downtown NO and the French Quarter to
pick up visitors before dropping us off at the airport. Then
upon return would bypass the University on I10 to take the
tourists to their destination first then double back to take us to
the campus. I mean the driver could've slowed down and we
could've jumped out of the van off the I10 ramp wearing our
backpacks! That's how close we were to the University.
Students began to complain to the drivers. Sometimes a
visiting passenger would chime in to convince a driver to
deliver us to our destination after hearing our moans. But it
never worked. The drivers would just repeat the same thing—
that they are instructed to drop *them* off first. I told one driver
we shouldn't be paying the same to be treated less than.

My first experience with this foolishness unfortunately led to
me to missing my first flight my freshman year. I booked
online and included my departure time. The shuttle service
determined the pick-up time based on that. I arranged to pay
in cash because I did not have a credit card in 1997 or a bank
card first semester of freshman year. So ill prepared to be so
far away from home. I paid the price for not carrying plastic
by my second semester. At the moment, at least, I did
everything I was supposed to do with the booking—
everything except be knowledgeable about the pick-up
process. I was the only student and first to be picked up the
day of my departure. Pick up was at a designated spot on

campus by the dorms. The driver greeted me and asked for my confirmation slip, money, and flight ticket before I hopped in. He loaded my carry-on luggage and I handed him the cash for the ride. He then gave me a receipt. The driver was nice during the ride, making all this small talk. Meanwhile, I notice we're driving east and not west to the airport. Without a smartphone, there was no update on my flight status or a digital itinerary for this "ride share" route I was on. You'd have to ask the driver,

"Where are you going?". And I did.

He informed me he had a route to downtown to get more passengers. He acted cool. So, I acted cool. We finally get to what was not downtown but the Business District for a pick up, then the Warehouse District, then downtown and turned on to the French Quarter for multiple stops at multiple hotels. Then I knew what this driver already knew when he saw my ticket—that I was definitely going to miss my first flight. I was furious but could not do a thing about it. I was almost in tears when I got to the American Airline concierge. But then I remembered the flight insurance my brother purchased. Thank God he was thinking of incidentals! The airline attendant rescheduled a later flight for that night to the Houston-Hobby airport where my layover was and phoned the Marriott airport hotel for an overnight stay as the next available connecting flight could only be scheduled for the next morning. I was in a funk when I got to the Airport Marriott in Houston not needing anymore mishaps for my first flight experience when one of the two men at concierge said that my hotel credit wasn't enough for the overnight stay.

"What?!" I yelled. "What do you mean not enough?!"

I'm panicking because I knew I didn't have enough cash to pay. And as I've revealed—no credit card. Thankfully, the guy next to him had a conscience and common sense pertaining to the nature of the matter and told me not to worry about it. My connecting flight was leaving early the same day as it was after 12 A.M. by then. I just needed to get to bed, any bed for a few hours. The sympathetic employee must have seen the distress on my face. I noticed he was also the same employee that brought my breakfast to my room 4 hours later. I got the vibe that he felt sorry for me. I needed *somebody* to feel sorry for me.

I believe a complaint was made to our school president about what we believed to be discriminatory practices of that shuttle service. I'm not sure what became of the situation. I started catching a ride to the airport by my sophomore year.

******

Traveling home by bus by far was the worst. My second freshman year roommate, Sharon, and I had to purchase tickets to take the bus home during winter break. I cannot remember how we got the tickets in the first place. But I definitely remember how I left my ticket in the dorm room in the second place. We were dropped off at the bus station and headed to the counter when I began reaching for my ticket in my purse. It wasn't there. Then I checked my jacket. It's not there. Then in a panic I stopped and checked my luggage.

"Ohhh-myyy-goodness! I don't have my ticket!" I yelled.

"You don't have your ticket?!" Sharon replied. "Check your

purse."

I checked again. "I remember picking it up! I remember picking it up and bringing it."

"Are you sure, Angie?"

"Yes. I remember picking it up!" (*yeah picking it up and sitting it right back down while packing* [eye roll emoji]).

No Plastic. I needed a credit card.

Sharon a week or two before was so elated about getting her first credit card. She probably got a free t-shirt too. I think the limit was $300. No job or any source of income required. Our line of credit otherwise known as student refund checks would suffice. She thought it was so great to have. I thought it was a big mistake. But it did remind me to call my parents to send my bank card.

Bank cards and debit cards were not exactly the same. A debit card typically attached to a Visa or Mastercard could be used anywhere Visa and Mastercard were accepted. Now mind you, back then, we had to ask merchants "Do you take Visa debit cards?" To which eventually a sign appeared at the McDonald's drive-thru, preemptively stating, "yeah, we take'em." It was new and cool to have because it was like having money in all the banks. But a bank card was just that, money in one bank. Maybe a merchant accepted your bank card. Maybe they didn't. Maybe you could use the closest ATM. Maybe you couldn't. Nobody in college could get by with 'maybe' money.

I found that out the hard way the day I left my bus ticket in the dorm room. I went to the ticket counter to tell the agent that I left my ticket. I anxiously step up to the counter and inform the agent of my situation, trying to get another ticket,

"What's your name?"

I told her.

"I see it here." She confirms.

"Good. Can you reprint it?"

"No. I'm not able to do that."

"Why not? It's right there. You can see that I have a ticket. Just print it."

"It doesn't work like that. You can't just reprint a ticket. You would have to purchase another one."

Why bother to search for my ticket if you can't reissue the ticket! My thoughts were screaming.

"Purchase another one?! You have got to be kidding me. It's right there. Just print it." I replied in frustration.

"I'm sorry. I can't."

I turned around looking everywhere then looked at my roommate.

"What am I gonna do?"

Whoever brought us to the station, possibly Chrissandra, dropped us off. We did NOT have cell phones in 1998.

"Why don't you call our pastor?" Sharon suggested as there were payphones. But neither one of us had his phone number with us.

"I have my check book!" I screamed like it was some fantastic idea.

I turned around towards the agent. "Can I write a check?"

"You can write it but I can't take it." She didn't say it that way but may as well have under the circumstances.

No plastic. Not nearly enough cash. No bank card that probably wouldn't have been accepted either. But my roomy had a brand-new Visa.

"Angie, you can use my credit card if you're sure you can pay me back."

"Oh my God! Yes! Yes, I can pay you back! Thank God you have a credit card!" I yelled in relief.

Sharon reluctantly, yet lovingly, handed over her shiny new Visa credit card that had only been used once previously to my knowledge by phone to order a Domino's pizza for the both of us. It was a budgeted two-person celebration of her new plastic financial freedom. She saved my butt that day. She hadn't had the card a full month and one-third of the limit had already been used. When we got on the bus I began writing a check for the amount. I reached over the back of her seat and gave it to her..

"Can I cash this when I get home?" She asked.

I'm thinking, *Why would I write a check that you couldn't cash?*

She's looking at the check.

"I have money. I just can't get to it." I responded to calm her worrying.

"Yes. You can cash it today, tomorrow, whenever you want to," I replied gratefully. I even added a few dollars in case she had to pay interest.

My bank card was in an envelope in my mailbox when we returned to campus after the break. *Maybe money.* Would you believe my parents still didn't get me a credit card after that debacle?

It took 2 years for me to open up an account at a national bank near the University. That was my junior year. It was then that I received my first Visa debit card.

******

The campus flooded my sophomore year at Xavier. I and hundreds of others were in class at the Norman C. Francis Science Building when out of nowhere announcements shuttered.

"Classes are canceled due to rain and flooding."

WHAT?

All I remember is a bunch of students including Measure and myself walking out onto the main campus and seeing water everywhere.

163

WHAT IN THE WORLD?

Students swarmed in every direction. Measure and I lived in the co-ed dorm that year, the LLC. It was located at Xavier South. Coming from the NCF building, we couldn't be any further from our destination. We used our only option. We walked. Water began covering our shoes. We walked further passing the pharmacy building. Water came up to our shins. More walking. Water crept up to our knees, then our thighs, then by the time we made it to the street between the Katherine Drexel and St. Mike's dormitories, the water was up to our waists. What could we do? Encourage each other and keep walking. It was absolutely crazy.

The canal adjacent to the University had reached its capacity and overflowed into the streets and neighborhoods. If you're familiar with NO, then you know it's a city-sized sink. Xavier sits in a sink within a sink, hence, the need for a canal next to it. We made it to the dorm soak and wet along with many others who *wade in the water*. No one was hurt as far as I knew. I found out later that Ron and several other smart students walked towards the east side of the campus, or maybe it's the north side. Alumni understand the directional dilemma there. XU South is actually East. The North campus is West. Anyway, Ron barely got wet in comparison. Again, no cell phones friends. Even if we did, smart phones had not been invented yet. No mobile weather alert. And a human, door-to-door intercom in the science building.

******

There were at least two hurricanes that hit New Orleans during my residence there. Students from out of state could not get over how the locals never panic. We panicked. We left. At least everyone I knew left. One year Annette and I headed to Hattiesburg, MS to seek refuge at Emerald's parents' house. Another year, Sharon, our classmate, Jamika, and myself high-tailed it out of NO heading towards Pine Bluff, AR where Jamika was from. We sped across the Lake Pontchartrain Causeway. Then teleported to Pine Bluff. Not really. But that's how afraid we were of the coming storm. None of us felt safe until we made it to dry land Arkansas. But the locals? They stayed. They always stay. Winds reached up to 155 mph, a category 4 before making landfall as a category 2. That was Hurricane Georges.

In about 7 years, Hurricane Georges would be eclipsed by Hurricane Katrina. It was devastating to say the least. Buses and trains left without passengers. No sufficient exit plan. People on top of roofs crying for help. The Super Dome turned into make-shift danger shelter. So many lives lost. The images were daunting. The reality of it was far worse. But I finally realized what I hadn't in college. Many people stay because they have nowhere to go. If a devastating storm hits, and it finally did, there was no home to flee to, no RV. For many, no money for an extended hotel stay. It was as if the collective governments, local, state and federal, solely depended on grace or luck all those years. No mass evacuation plan for a city that is 2 to 10 ft below sea level, sitting right in the mouth of the Mississippi Gulf. Everyone failed New Orleans and the surrounding area.

I failed people I knew and loved. Doing something is always better than doing nothing. I was 2 years post-grad, working, married, in my 3rd trimester, and had a toddler. I couldn't tell night from day on some days. I used to look back and think,

Why didn't Ron and I do something?. That was our home away from home. We had adopted family there. I actually do not remember calling anyone. If I didn't have their contact info, I could've found it had I tried. I do not remember trying. But I do remember our lives back then, being in the middle of a proverbial hurricane within our own home. Real life was kicking my butt. We were battling our own storm. Ron and I were in survival mode, coping with our own mess. I'm not making an excuse. I'm telling the truth. We had nothing left to give.

******

Who didn't have suitemates on campus? If you spend at least 6 years in college, you're bound to share your space with at least one. I had eight. One being a rogue, who I inherited by moving in a year after her. That was my senior year of college and 2nd year of pharmacy school. I noticed money missing from my desk drawer in my dorm room. I didn't usually leave cash in my room but did this time for some reason. It was there for days. Well, one morning I happen to reach for the cash and noticed $20 missing. You know how you can doubt yourself, thinking, *Did I? Or maybe I didn't. Maybe I only placed $60 in the drawer* (thinking emoji). But I didn't. It was $80. Four 20-dollar-bills. I called Ron and asked him if he remembered seeing the money in my drawer.

"There's a 20 missing from my desk drawer. I told him. "Did you happen to go in it. It was $80 total."

"So, I stole it?" He asked, in offence.

"I wasn't accusing you. I need someone else to have seen it

so that I can have a witness. Or at least know that I'm not crazy!"

Males were NOT allowed in those rooms, by the way, only the common areas. But the dorm mothers loooooved Ron. Ron always came in my room. No one ever checked to find out otherwise. Plus, what roommate wants to see your guy in the common space all the time? Not that he was there all the time. But he was there a lot (grinning face emoji).

So, Ron was no help. I couldn't have used him as a witness anyway. Still, I knew someone stole from me. There was one exit. One common space. One bath. Two suitemates. One of them, Suitemate #1, was always in her room. The other, Sheila (Suitemate #2), also a pharmacy major and a year ahead of me, was just as busy as me. She was in-and-out, like me. She later moved out without any warning. Not even a goodbye. Then a 3rd suitemate took Sheila's room. She was nice at first. But then became not so nice abruptly and stopped speaking to me.

Fast-forward.

One night all dressed up in a sleeveless double-breasted, navy-blue pant suit, I returned to the dorm worn out after attending some social event. I walked slowly in pumps with sore legs and feet up the two long flights of stairs. The one time I wished I lived on the first floor. Then half-way up, out pops my old suitemate that moved out. She lived a floor below me now.

"Angie, you got a minute?"

I paused, looking up at her three steps from landing on the 2nd

floor, seeing half of her standing between the door and her suite. I turned my head and closed my eyes for 3 seconds, then stared right at her with a knowing expression.

"Sheila, if you're about to say what I think you're about to say, I am going to have a fit." I responded tired and tensing up. "You were missing money too," I said with assurance.

"Yep," Sheila said while nodding. She invited me in.

Sheila gave me the whole overdue narrative about how she was missing cash but didn't know who to accuse. That was understandable. She reported her missing cash to our dorm mother. I never did. Not realizing I was being monitored along with Suitemate #1. I gave Sheila my story. We both commented on how we could not understand how one suitemate could afford Domino's pizza delivered so often. Like up to 3 times a week! So right there we figured out it was Suitemate #1. Sheila talked about how she would have helped her out if she had asked.

"I wouldn't have mind! She didn't have to steal from me!" She insisted.

I, in hood fashion, acted out how I would have gone upside her head with an iron if I had known. The nerve! I can tolerate a liar better than I can tolerate a thief. Smiling in my face every time she saw me. Even having conversations in passing. I informed Suitemate #3 when I got to the room. She was at least saying "hi" to me by then, comfortable enough to step out of her room when I knocked on her door. She did not have to be convinced.

"My debit card was missing! Then it later magically returned right where I left it," she said pointing to the floor where a folder was laying. "That's why I used the talc powder. I sprinkled it on the floor in front of my door."

"I remember seeing that," I admitted with a smirk. Now knowing why.

The thief wasn't to be caught that way though. She was smarter than that. What the other two suitemates couldn't figure out was how she got into our bedrooms without us knowing. We concluded in part that the theft occurred while we were taking showers. The only time we would not lock our doors. But then I had to confess that I'd learned from an RA how to break into my room if I left my key. They charged students a fee if they locked themselves out of their bedrooms. A dorm mother or an RA had a master key and unlocked it for you. It only took a spreading knife to get in if you maneuvered it the right way in between the lock and closure. I had to use that trick once. Unfortunately, I recalled while confessing that Suitemate #1 saw me at the time while she was going into her room. But she paused just long enough to see the trick work. Pretending as if she was trying to find her own key or was having trouble with the lock. I wasn't cognizant enough to notice that she was lingering to observe me —20/20 in hindsight.

Neither of us got the chance to confront her. She finished her academic program a semester early never returning to be held accountable. And to think how this thief hounded me about a pair of scissors I borrowed from her.

I had two additional suitemates after that. Staying on campus proved to be a luxury I wasn't so eagerly ready to relinquish.

Suitemate #4 caught an STI early in the school year. She was so confused as to how she contracted it. She hadn't had sex with any guy.

"I don't know how I got it? I only kissed them." She told me while holding her abdomen.

Suitemate #5 was from the upper East Coast. She was some sort of genius to my understanding about her. Cool and down to earth. But also high strung. For whatever reason after moving in, she told me about this pesticide called "La bamba" and how it got rid of monster roaches. *I've never seen a monster roach in here and I better not see one after you move in.* I was thinking while staring at her.

"We don't have roaches. I don't think you have anything to worry about," I assured her.

I noticed she walked fast even in the hallways. She disappeared out the door after our conversation. What a weird thing to tell someone after a meet and greet.

Fast-forward.

Weeks later I came back from Thanksgiving break unwound, having all but forgotten a tough semester. But the semester ain't over. It's back to business. I unlocked the door to the common space living area. There was white powder everywhere. All over the floor. All over the walls. On the furniture and the doors.

"What the hell?!" I do a 360 after closing the main door.

"What is this?! What is all this?! What happened?!"

Apparently yelling at no one since no one appeared from their room.

I put my things in my room then went back downstairs to speak with the dorm mother but I don't recall if she was aware of what happened or was protecting someone out of respect for their privacy. I called a friend, then my mom. Then at some point Suitemate #4 came in. She told me it was Suitemate #5. The dialog went something like this:

"I think she lost it. Rambling. Saying something about roaches being everywhere. I didn't see any roaches," she said with a baffled expression on her face looking around the room.

"It's La bamba," I said to myself but out loud.

"La' what?" Suitemate #4 replied even more confused. She continued, "I mean poured that stuff everywhere! I didn't know what was happening! It's all over the place. I think she had a nervous breakdown."

Weeks later I returned to the suite to see her father packing her things. She never returned after the incident. I introduced myself.

"Oh, hello!" He chimed.

"How is she doing? Is... is she alright?"

"She's ok but not ok. You know what I mean?" He said, pausing to pick up books and shrugging his shoulders to answer.

"Well let her know we're thinking about her and we miss her." I added.

The news about her was already trickling around campus. I don't know for sure but it was said that she had a pre-existing mental disorder and had a relapse in the aftermath of 9/11.

******

I became the news on campus soon enough …. Ron proposed on Halloween of 2002. We found out we were expecting in mid-January 2003. Prior to that, I had been home visiting my folks on Christmas break with an upset stomach. Nothing tasted right. I was complaining the whole time of malaise and I didn't eat much while there. My brother gave me Crown and Coke to settle my stomach. Not once did it cross my mind during Christmas vacation that I was pregnant. That thought came to mind when Ron drove from Georgia to visit me in January. Because we were up to no good again. That is when it hit me. My period hadn't come in at least two months. Any female college student can tell you that's not uncommon. Life is stressful. It happens. But this was life on a whole-other level. Everything, the trajectory of our lives, whatever plans we had, it all changed with a positive pink double line on a pee pee stick.

I was sick as a dog every-freaking-day. I didn't have morning sickness. I suffered all-day sickness. In the morning, driving on the way to rotations, driving back home from rotations and before bed. Please understand that even though baby-making out of wedlock (showing my age) was quite common back then, I had no plans of joining that club. After all, I had made it out of high school baby-free. I mean as far as high school

was concerned, you were in the minority if you didn't have a
baby back then. Younger Gen Xers were over-exposed and
undereducated. I mean we watched tv and listened to all that
had everything to do with sex-laced, bump-and-grind
influential music being played on the radio all the time. It was
like an anthem in the 90s. It was unavoidable. Oh, the
hypocrisy of our ridicule of hypersexualized music artists
these days!

Anyway, Black students just did it uninhibited. No
commitment required. White students did it but married right
after high school. Many divorced soon after, though. Who
knows anything about love at that age? Hardly anyone. But
we all knew *Wanderlust*!

Wanderlust lives on co-ed college campuses and for many
during high school. I wish I had met the young lady; that
college student who persevered four or more years and
resisted Wanderlust in the name of Jesus. How? I, too, was a
Christian college student (angel face, Bible emoji). I wish I
was Yvonne Orji. I mean it's one thing if you've never been
pursued. Anybody can remain a virgin when nobody's
checking for you. But what college girl doesn't get
pressured? I mean, pursued? No pq? I mean, never?! I'd like
to meet her. Wish I had met her—the spiritually mature
young woman in college. 'Cause I was NOT that chick!

Nonetheless, I was a late bloomer in every way. Nearly
everyone had done the nasty by high school graduation. As
for myself, nothing was worth commenting on prior to my
Boo. It's always the ones you least expect. Two quiet people
getting it on and on and on. Oh, the places! The nerve! The
excursions! The impromptu great escapes! We were doing the

most! And we paid the price. Over at the Red Roof Inn when we should've been at the Bayou Classic.

**Quick note here, smart readers. A little word of advice because I just can't help myself. Know this; God's Plan is the best plan. He made these rules, you see, a long, long, long, time ago. Because when left to our own devices we make bad decisions. So, He set up these guardrails to protect us from bad things that existed long before we got here. At times, those guardrails even protect us from us. We may not understand it. We may even defy it. But we will certainly pay the price when we do.

I have always believed that my life has divine favor. I, and you, are given grace upon grace whether we acknowledge it or not. But undermining God's Plan has consequences. Ron and I kept knocking over those guardrails until consequence caught up with us. Whatever your age, a word of advice, stick to The Master's Plan.

13

Kappa What??

Ron escorted me to the Pharmacy Ball in the Spring of 2000. One of his close friends, Morris, who he jokingly nicknamed "Mo the Ho," let Ron borrow his formal wear. Ron told me he didn't have anything in his closet that was suitable to wear to the ball. The suit was black with a white dress shirt and purple vest with paisley-looking designs in it. I thought the suit was fly. He and Morris were about the same size so the clothes fit quite nicely. I wore a simple velvet spaghetti strapped black gown with a folded neckline slightly adorned with rhinestones. The black shawl I wore with it was borrowed from one of my Kappa Psi brothers, Kelly, a female by the way. The concept of an organization including members who are women recognized as *brothers* gets a little confusing. Kelly and another *brother,* Brittney, were a part of the royal court at the XUCOP that year. The court wore silver gowns and gloves that year. The Pharmacy Ball was the one event outside of undergrad celebrations that a lot of students looked forward to. It was repeated numerous times back then that the Pharmacy Ball was better than the University's Coronation Ball. I imagine it was due to stressed out, overworked, and underpaid soon to be Doctors of Pharmacy who unleashed every bit of celebratory fiber in their burned-out bodies during the final leg of their very expensive scholastic careers. That would be 2 semesters of mostly clinical rotations by year 4 or 6 depending on when and where you started. Some rotations were so long that you never saw the sun. P4s were also working while studying for licensing exams, if you were being responsible. I can assure you, we'd had enough of pharmacy school by then.

We arrived at the ball at a reasonable time. I found our table full of KPsi brothers. I was making my way around the ballroom some time later after the royal court was announced, when I stopped to meet Brittney's parents. Her father was either a police chief or sheriff in Natchez, MS from what I recall. That introduction turned out to be an awkward encounter. I introduced myself. Brittney's father looked at her and laughed at either my place of origin, which was Arkansas, or my twang that followed me all the way from Arkansas to pharmacy school. I glanced at Brittney who seemed a bit embarrassed by her dad's belittling. I smiled at him. Then smiled at her with sympathy in a *you can't control what your father does any more than I can control what my father does* kinda way. I told him it was nice meeting him. Then I politely kept it moving. I went to complement Kelly, poked my nose into other people's conversations, then joined my brothers for a group photo. There were about 12 of us. I must say we all looked good. I still have the photo.

At some point the Pharmacy Ball lived up to its rep. Fourth year COP students with no shame, faculty and undergrads who were not invited got their groove on. I danced at least once with Ron. Before that he sat stationary at our group table practically bent over the table cloth. I wished he would sit up properly. He only spoke when spoken to adding a smile for good measure. I gave him a warm grin hoping that would alleviate any feelings of being uncomfortable. He was eventually spotted by Lawrence, a mutual friend from undergrad. Lawrence was that guy in undergrad that was everywhere, knew everyone and seemed to be involved in everything on campus. They're still friends today. Lawrence was definitely someone Ron could let his guard down with and talk to. I was relieved. Otherwise, he would've barely engaged in any conversation that whole night. Not that I'd complain. His only job was to look handsome and he succeeded. He was so shy. Our former Regent, August, who I'm pretty sure would normally balk at bashfulness, had to admit in a whisper leaning towards my ear,

"He's so cute!"

My dapper date and I left arm in arm before the elegant evening concluded.

That shawl I borrowed still wrapped around my shoulders mysteriously snagged itself on something. At least that's the story I'm sticking to. Why can't some people return things the way they were given? I handed it back to Kelly on another day neatly folded. My face was gleaming as I glided away before she realized the snag. I did so with the same innocent smile two years later when returning my rented princess-style wedding dress to the boutique, filthy along the train from grass and mud I stepped in after my rain-soaked wedding.

I must've been circulating quite a bit at the ball. My feet hurt so bad by the time we left. I must have also been complaining while walking so awkwardly. No more ballroom pretty girl walk. It felt like *Crush Groove* in my shoes. Even worse we were nowhere near Ron's car that was parked way too far in the parking deck across the street. I don't know if it was my facial expression, my pigeon-toed limp, or something I said. But Ron must've gotten the message. Right before my legs gave up, he bent towards me with open-arms and swept me right off my feet. From there he proceeded to carry me from one side of the parking deck to the other while I wrapped my arms around his shoulders. I leaned into him. What a moment. I was grinning from ear to ear, feeling like a rescued pigeon-toed princess; elated to say the least. I wasn't heavy. But neither was I as light as a feather. This was our senior year. I was well beyond the freshman 15 by then. It was the perfect exit from a royal evening.

******

Now about my sisters Kelly and Brittney being my *brothers*… Believe it or not, there is a such thing as a co-ed fraternity in pharmacy school. Xavier had two: Kappa Psi and Kappa Epsilon. Why they exist, I'm not so sure. It served equally as an outlet and a distraction. Who has time to join professional Pan-Hellenic organizations on top of other way more important pursuits? Long-story short, in my case, it was self-induced misguidance.

Early in the first year of pharmacy school, representatives from all of the active organizations were on display. It was the annual organizational fair held in the main lobby and hallway of the pharmacy building. I loved campus involvement and volunteering so I knew I would join something. I made my way around each table set up to impress, not necessarily introducing myself, listening to what each organization had to offer. I made it my business to gather pamphlets which came in handy in case I didn't remember a word that was said in such a loud and slightly crowded space. People *were* trying to get to class in the middle of it all. I collected info about PSA (Pharmacy Student Association) that technically every student is a member of, a leadership society that I can't remember the name of but I did join the next year, Rho Chi (the high achievement honor society that I never qualified for), a fraternity that no men joined (Kappa Epsilon), and a couple more. Then I turned the corner to the right where a table was practically blocking the main hallway. There were 3 or 4 young women sitting at the table dressed professionally. Two of them I would later find out were from my home state and became friends with. But in the moment as I looked above them, I saw at least 4 of the finest men I'd ever seen in the pharmacy building. All tall, clean-cut and dreamy. I didn't know who they were outside of the fresh attire they wore that day. But at this moment they were all the men from the movie *The Best Man*. They wore dark suits, one of them wore a long-sleeved white dress shirt, no jacket. They all had swag, boasting pressed grey and/or red ties I later found out represented their organizational colors. I'm sure I was staring at them forgetting all about the women in front of them. As I walked closer, eyes glowing by now, I thought, '*Who are you and how can I be down?!*'. The introduction to my future fraternity brothers went something that crescendoed verbally like,

"Who are you all?" I'm smiling, not hearing the answer but mouths were moving.

"I'm..." Maybe I said Angie. Maybe I said Esther.

"Kappa Psi?" Looking confused. *Isn't that a fraternity for male undergrads?*

They explained.

"Okay!" I picked up a pen and gave all of my contact info to a group of strangers.

And just like that, blinded by attractive men, I signed up for the interest meeting. I got a better look at all of the members at the meeting. Everyone seemed cool and inviting. They introduced themselves one by one. I found out many of them had degrees already and pledged social Pan-Hellenic organizations. I should have taken that as a warning sign. *Get Out! Now!* We became better acquainted during the interest meeting, playing a game of name association. I was "awesome" Angie. It was a cool meet and greet. If *I chose them*, I believed I'd fit in well. There were quite a few interested first and second-year pharmacy students. That number dwindled by the time *they chose us*. The chosen ones were later interviewed and subsequently called to assemble. They were a real fraternity with a real history dating back to 1879. Men and eventually women were inducted during a secret formal ceremony into membership. The campus Delta Eta chapter had a recorded history of past members, even the first white pledge member. And yes, they actually pledged! This is Pharmacy School. Are they for real?! Yes. Yes, they were. I can't remember how many began the process. But I do remember that the total number dwindled to 4, 1 male, 3 females. We dressed in uniform with pill boxes stringed around our necks made of match boxes where we stored notes from countless amounts of information obtained during pledging that we could not possibly store in our brains alongside Biochemistry, Medical Terminology, Pharmacology, etc. Along with class notes and reading material we jammed packed into our brains before we set foot in a space where we were constantly quizzed about founders and quoting Pan-Hellenic history that dated back to the late 1800s. This was ridiculousness! The men were decoys! I was tricked! But I stepped in it. Quitting was not in my vocab back then. So, I had to finish it. At the most I'd gain new relationships and hopefully favor towards my prospective career. At the least, well, I'm surrounded by handsome men, albeit I didn't have a chance at dating any of them (sad face emoji). But I'd be right next to them (happy face emoji). We'd go out to social gatherings. I'd be talking to them all the while they had no clue as to what I was thinking. Why couldn't Ron be a pharmacy major? I had 2 additional years of curriculum than he did. Two years of separation from this man. How in the world did we make this relationship work? It must be love.

If I omit the pledge process, I have to say that everyone was super cool, even the mean ones. Everyone sincerely wanted everyone to succeed. It was a good vibe amongst men and women, no shady people that I could recall. Tolerating my big brothers gave me the courage to run for class president the next year. I won. No one ran against me (lol emoji). Subsequently, I became Dean of Pledges, treasurer of one organization, a charter member of the campus Toast Masters, and became Vice Regent of KPsi only because I lost the Regent position to my fellow Arkansan and friend, Theresa. No bad blood. I did become Regent the next year, though.

******

The following years of pharmacy school after I joined KPsi, we pledge three additional groups. The first group named themselves "Nitrous Oxide." They were 4 clowns. All of them my classmates that made it to the pledging process. I lovingly call them "clowns." They really kept us laughing which made it more difficult when we had to get down to business. We showed up at one of their apartments to let them all have it for what we perceived to be them slacking off. For whatever reason, I had a remote in my hand while berating them. In the middle of my pretend fit, I'm sure I gently tossed the remote on the floor during the verbal rant. That's how I remembered it. Somehow the remote broke. I tried to play it off but two of my brothers were making a big deal out of it.

"You broke it!," they both said laughing but serious at the same time.

"Girl, you broke his remote control!" Theresa picked up the parts off the floor.

Just play along. I'm trying to convey my thoughts to these two. *I can't look apologetic in front of the pledges.* One pledge, Arvie, who's apartment we were in, and who's remote I broke, looked concerned to say the least. He didn't say anything, just stared at his broken property. But my disposition did not change. I acted like Rick James tracking dirt on a couch in that classic episode of "Chappelle's Show," *F... yo remote!* It was a Sanyo remote control. *I can get those for free. One of my relatives works for the company.* I thought to myself. No big deal. As long as those clowns took me seriously. Theresa and Kam, my Arkansan brothers and forever friends, made me apologize a few days later.

My last year of leadership, the year I served poorly as
Regent, we had somewhere between 13 to 17 pledges. They
had my undivided attention until they didn't. That was my P4
year. My last year of pharmacy school! My head was so far
out the door. Not long after we began, our Vice Regent,
Donna, and Arvie, the Dean of Pledges that year, had to take
over. They understood as I had a little too much going on at
the time. P4 students were focused on rotations and preparing
for our licensing exams if we were being responsible. Many
if not all of us were working to make sure we could afford
those licensing exams and the next major U-Haul move, if we
were being responsible. We had rotations, mostly clinical that
began way too early in the morning or finished way too late
in the evening. Plus, I was making wedding plans in the
middle of all that. And I was pregnant.

******

Sadly, in the fall of the year I graduated, one of our brothers
who I'll refer to as "Jay" was tragically murdered in Atlanta.
My friend, Adam, one of the brothers I pledged with, tried to
call me right after finding out about it. But I'd left my cell
phone at my apartment when driving to my parents' house to
visit 6 hours away. When I returned, I saw that he'd left a
message. I called him back.

"Hey." He sounded a little somber.

"Hey Adam! How's it going?"

"Did you hear about Jay? I tried calling you [and some
others]. You didn't pick up. I couldn't get anyone. No one

wanted to talk about it."

I explained to him that I was out of town and accidently left my cell.

"I can't believe this happened," I said.

"I know," he said. "Me either."

Theresa, who I spoke with soon after, attended Jay's funeral along with at least a few other KPsi brothers and presented a plaque to his family. She filled me in during that conversation of the brief, but devastating details.

"Jay had moved back to his old neighborhood where he lived with his mother after he graduated. One day he went over to a childhood friend's house nearby to play video games when a gunman rushed in and shot his friend and Jay at point blank range, killing both of them. The gunman was [reportedly] after his friend," Theresa was told. Jay just happened to be in the wrong place at the wrong time. Everyone I spoke with was in shock. I can only imagine how crushed his family was, especially his mother. He had only been a pharmacist one year when his life was taken violently.

******

I kept in contact with my brothers for a little while post-graduation by phone, then text, then Facebook. Then years went by. Then life does what it does; reprioritizes. I received a FB invite from a fraternity member, Ravin, one of my line brothers who's also an author now, to join a KPsi group chat. I didn't respond. Plus, I had moved on to IG by then. I once got a phone call late one night asking if I'd return to campus for that year's pledge process. *Do you know what time it is? Do you have a job?* That was college life. Things are different now. I live in the real world. I think I began to naturally distance myself. Then I gave up Kappa everything after stepping into the ministry. It's all a memory now.

PART III:
THE BREAKING
POINT

14

Welcome to "Methingham" County

In 2008 my husband finally landed a job with a sought-after Georgia based company in the Low Country. That was the good news. The bad news was that we had to leave the Atlanta suburbs to live deeper into the deep Southern state. Geographically, the butt of the state of Georgia; or the pot belly of the state depending on which way you shift your view. Either way, we were embarking on a part of the state that was out of touch and swollen with ideologies of the past.

The best news was that I still had a job. Back then, if you worked for the top two major pharmacy chains, the process for finding a job was as simple as sending a couple of emails to two district supervisors within the same chain. One email to the current boss that says "I'm leaving." Another email to the future boss that says "I'm coming." And that was that. A job was waiting for me when I got to Whatever Town, Georgia. So, with two toddlers in tow, we relocated to the

outskirts of Savannah, GA in a rural town called Rincon. "Stinkin' Rincon" was its nickname. Most of its residents lived within a few miles of at least three chemical plants. One of the plants was a paper mill. Anyone that has lived anywhere near a paper mill can tell you it stinks in the worst way. A person could get dementia and would never forget the scent of that funk. It penetrates from the nostrils to the stomach. In Rincon, the smell would latch into the air from the plant 1 or 2 days a month. That was more than enough. For the life of me I could not understand how it was tolerated for so long by residents. Accept that it was legal.

When considered, residents should've realized there were an unusual number of questionable environmental concerns in Rincon. Soon after moving there, I noticed the heavy chlorine that was used periodically to "clean" the tap water in homes. Nothing abnormal about that except that the water had an otherwise odd taste that we never got used to. While working in the pharmacy there, I noticed the tap water from time to time would get an odor. When I asked management about it, I was told it was sulfur. Why is there detectable sulfur in tap water? Where did it come from? Now the water that was used for compounding and reconstituting powder antibiotics underwent a filtration process prior to dispensing. But if you work there, oh well, drink up. At least 3 female employees had the same concerning health issue within 2 years of working there. Another employee was diagnosed with cancer during the same time span.

I researched the cancer rate for the area. It was about the same as the national average. But high for the state. When I compared it to metro Atlanta areas, the one thing in contrast were the locations of chemical plants. Cancer rates were higher in counties where chemical plants were concentrated. For instance, Gwinnett County had a cancer rate much less in 2008 than the national average and less than that part of the state. Whereas Effingham County had a cancer rate much higher than Gwinnett. I'm not certain if it's a matter of how many chemical plants exist within the two counties or if it is a matter of how chemical waste is released and disposed of. But Effingham County? Ya got a problem.

Those unfortunate cases among fellow employees could very well have been unrelated in terms of their causes. But it gave me no comfort that they were all in proximity to polluted air and tainted water.

At some point while living in Effingham County I developed some skin infection that appeared to come out of nowhere. It would start as an itchy bump that looked like an allergic rash. After a few days the bump would flatten, appearing necrotic and turning near black as if my skin was breaking down from some sort of bacterial infection. Then it disappeared in a week or so.

"What the freak is this?"

I shared the experience of my "necrosis" with a manager at one of the pharmacies I frequently worked in. With wide eyes I listened to him give the same description of what I experienced. It appeared on his hand and arms recently.

"What is it and where is it coming from?" I asked him. He didn't know.

I didn't bother to tell anyone else about it other than a dermatologist. The nurse practitioner there took a razor blade and sliced off a few layers of infected flesh a millimeter wideto be viewed under a microscope. She determined the rash to be a fungal infection called dermatophytosis. A year or so later, a dermatologist I saw in Douglas Co. disputed the diagnosis. The nurse practitioner asked if I had been planting or had my hands in dirt lately. I had planted pink double knockout roses on the front lawn weeks ago. The soil of course has phosphorus in it among other minerals and could have caused the infection. However, after a fellow employee made the same claim about the same irritable rash, I was more inclined to the alternative conclusion that it came from touching dirty money exchanged from dirty hands that had been working in dirty places, like shipping ports and chemical plants.

******

It wasn't uncommon to encounter plant workers, my husband being one of them. They were compensated handsomely and rightfully so. The jobs and the work environments were dangerous. The most devastating catastrophe to date occurred in February 2008 in nearby Port Wentworth. Fourteen employees were killed in the Imperial Sugar Company refinery explosion. A total of 40 were injured. At least one of the survivors, once released from the hospital, came to the drive-thru at the pharmacy. His wife was driving. I saw him on the passenger side. Most of his head was bandaged and one of his arms was wrapped in bandages. I could see his scarred eyes and burns on the right side of his face as he turned my way. I exchanged greetings and smiled in an empathetic fashion making sure not to stare. He was so young. Then I looked down to grab the handle of the drive thru drawer delivering the bagged prescriptions that were paid for in full by either our company for the refinery. Either way we definitely never charged any of the victims that chose to get their medications with us. It was an up-close reality of that horrible accident. What was more unnerving was knowing that it all could have been prevented. The explosion was ignited by combustible sugar dust left unremoved in the outdated facility by contract maintenance workers. It was pure negligence.

My husband, Ron, was a Senior EHS Specialist at the time who often has the repetitive task of preventing and correcting potential hazards in the workplace like the one that caused the Port Wentworth tragedy. It serves as another underappreciated job. My older sister, Rachelle, joked that he tells people, "to go and wash their hands". As funny as that is, it's hardly the case. He's more like Smokey the Bear. He politely trains, audits and corrects the troops, aka employees. However, the natural response of the troops is to resist compliance measures. No one wants to be told what to do or how to do it. But it is literally his job to tell people what to do, how to do it and what not to do as it pertains to safety.

The cute thing about Smokey is that he presents himself as this people friendly, giant teddy bear in blue trousers and a ranger's hat. In actuality, Smokey's a 7ft tall brown grizzly bear that could claw your face off! Ron's the nicest guy you've never met. He's 5'10" or so, thin and looks damn good in a custom-made suit. He's mild mannered and patient, always wanting to be Smokey in the baggy trousers. But lack of care and concern for safety by employees cause him to rip off the trousers on rare occasions. Respect for the role only occurs when disaster happens. Disaster can range from a huge liquid spill to negligible death. That horrible explosion in Port

Wentworth is a heart heavy reminder of just how important the EHS position is.

******

Now I dare not claim to be Mrs. Clean, however, I offer no exaggeration when I say that some people who approach the retail counter in that region were unbelievably dirty. Dirty hands, dirty money, dirty debit cards. Exhibit A: I cannot count the number of times a grown man came to pick up a prescription with the nastiest hands. Nails brown and black, fingers and palms smutty. And the so and so's have the audacity to hand over cash just as filthy as their fingertips.

I remember one creepy guy who wore dirt from his curly hair to his pink toes every time he came to the pharmacy. He was excessively nice and grinned too much. We were giving flu shots so I was inclined to ask him if he wanted one. To my dismay he said yes. I didn't trust the guy especially after he offered me candy one day when I was working alone. He reached his long grimy arm across the counter to hand it to me. I could not believe he expected me to take it from his filthy hand. But I did like a dummy not wanting to hurt a kind customer's feelings. But I should've hurt his feelings. The guy kept coming back when I worked alone. So, the day I gave him the flu shot I called the store manager to the pharmacy to be there with me. We had a designated room to give immunizations and there was no way I was going to be in an enclosed space with this guy. For all I know, he could've given me the dermato-whatever fungus cooties I caught while working there. Til this day I have some hyper skin reaction to certain foods that I believe was ignited by that fungal infection. Thanks to that experience and a diuretic prescribed to me, I wash my hands religiously up to 15 times a day.

On another nasty note, Exhibit B: I was working a Saturday shift in Garden City. Garden City is a town in between Rincon and Savannah where the company planted a store enroute to the two places. I was working a pretty busy shift alone as usual. Typically, a technician was scheduled to come in later. I was typing on my computer when one of the front cashiers, an Indian American young lady, who appeared a bit irritated, came to the consult window with a perfume bottle. She almost slammed the bottle on the counter.

"She was trying to steal this," she told me. Then she turned to eyeball the culprit and walked away. She took it from a customer who was clearly trying to stuff it on her person. The customer, a disheveled heavy blonde woman possibly in her late 50s, cursed at her. She was as dingy and dirty as her mouth. She then yelled towards the cashier,

"I wasn't trying to steal anythang! I was gonna gittit at the pharmacy!"

The woman seemed to be using her sweat pants as a shopping cart. Some customers don't want to shop with a store basket. They'd rather fill their hands, arms and sweat pants with goods from the aisles. It can be an unnecessary burden. We like to help those customers out. So, the cashier explained that she was providing extra customer care by bringing the perfume to the pharmacy for her to lighten her load. When she and her equally dingy compadre made it to the pharmacy I asked with an insincere smile,

"Are you picking up a prescription?"

She wasn't. She simply chose to purchase her items all the way in the back of the store; at the pharmacy. The other lady she was with left to get something else. I think the cashier followed her from the opposite end of the aisles. I went back to my computer until they got it together. Just when I turned to walk back over a few minutes later, I see the would-be thief who was still waiting for her friend, stretch out her red sweatpants, reach down into the pit of her underwear and pull out a wad of cash! My face looked like I'd just tasted the worst vegetable in the world.

"Oh my God!"

I made a beeline to the back of the pharmacy for the purple vinyl gloves we used for giving flu shots.

"Who does that?!"

I'm whispering obscenities while struggling to put the gloves on in a hurry. Her bare hands slid down under to her bare twat where she stashed her bare cash! So, I reiterate, some people across that counter can be downright filthy. You would have thought I was headed to perform an incision with surgical gloves on, walking with my arms up and fingers spread, palms at shoulder length as I headed back to the register. But then….. as I resurfaced to take the twatted twenty-dollar bill, another front-end cashier, our standby when we get overwhelmed at check out, was placing the booty buck in the till and giving the dingy woman and her dingy friend their change.

"Abby Nooooo! Oh my God!" I choked!

It was too late! They took their bagged goods and change and left.

"Abby," I said in my most calm voice,

"Hey! I didn't see your tech. I came to help out," she stated in such a chipper tone all bright eyed.

"Go wash your hands."

"What?"

"Go-and-wash-your-hands...now," I said in a frozen circumstance of disbelief of what just happened.

I was dumbfounded. Abby was just confused. But did as I told her. Later, I found out those two women were kleptos who frequented that location. I guess employees never call the police. So, they kept coming back.

******

That location was a spooky spot at night. I often called someone, my husband or a sibling when I felt a little unsafe. I don't consider it unfounded. One of the 24-hour locations a few miles away in Savannah was robbed one night by a drive-thru bandit. The overnight pharmacist in her first year of practice was working there alone when it happened. I'm sure I would've quit after that. Fresh out of pharmacy school, I'm sure *she* didn't.

******

I was on the phone with my older brother, Macon, in Garden City one night, working alone there as a pharmacist often did after dark at that location. Two men walked in that I had never seen before. They appeared to be in their 30s, two shades of brown skin, tall and thin. They would have otherwise been mistaken for the contract maintenance workers the way they paced the floors. Except they had no brooms or buffers. Neither were they shopping. Then they both stopped at the pharmacy looking right and left then at each other. I told my brother in a low voice,

"Hey, I'm in the pharmacy in Garden City on Highway 21. These two dudes walked in acting funny. I'm here by myself. Call 911 if the phone hangs up. Otherwise, don't hang up."

One of the men leaned over the consult window. His eyes were big and red, like after drinking too much liquor or inhaling weed, red. But definitely not 'I'm sleep deprived' red. I held the phone closer to my face. He leaned all the way in, making me seriously uncomfortable. He looked from one side of the pharmacy to the next as if to make sure no one else was there. I froze. My brother must have frozen too because he didn't say a word.

"Can I help you with something, sir?"

I asked him while gripping the phone and not once blinking. The other guy he was with was at the register counter waiting. I just braced for whatever was about to happen. The man leaning over the consult window a few feet in front of me who again looked towards the far end of the pharmacy as if to make certain there was just me, finally asked a question.

"Do you have something for my eyes? Some drops?"

I don't know what I told him. I don't know if it was the fear in my eyes, my stiff stance or me gripping the phone that made the difference. But he slowly backed away from the window then looked at me with suspicion as he walked away from the counter. His friend followed. They left the store. Then I hear my brother,

"You ok?"

"Yeah. They're gone."

I could've very well been overly paranoid. But I'd rather be that than scared stupid because two men hopped the pharmacy counter demanding whatever because they saw a petite and defenseless young female employee working alone and seized an opportunity.

******

By circumstance, I had a stalker at the same location. He "relocated" to the area from Florida. I found out later he was homeless. The fellow was one of many homeless people bussed to Savannah from Florida. Back then, city authorities like the Jacksonville PD had an unwelcoming habit of purchasing one way bus tickets and mailing their homeless residents who were considered a nuisance, across the border to Georgia. Heartless. Anyway, the man had plenty of prescriptions to be filled but no insurance card. He said he didn't have any insurance when asked. I didn't want him to go without his meds, so I told him we'd figure something out. Besides a discount card I really wasn't sure what we could do. But to buy time I told him to give us a day or two to work on it. He agreed to return on another day. Long story short, I retrieved his social security number from the medical office that he visited and found out he had Medicare Part B. I don't know who thought that was a good idea to have social security numbers on those red, white and blue cards as so many identifications were stolen over the years. But in this instance, it was super helpful as we had the capacity to search for active prescription insurance coverage. Turns out he also had Medicare Part D (à la George W. Bush). *Thank God* is what I was thinking. So, instead of disappointing our new resident upon his return, he was blessed with about a 95% discount. He was so happy handing us those dirty dollars to put in the till in exchange for a boatload of new medications. When I returned on my next shift, I found that he'd left a thank you card.

"What a kind gesture of appreciation." I said something like that, smiling.

 The pharmacy manager, a tall and thin white female a couple of years younger than me, who really took care of herself, told me,

"He's come back here a few times looking for you."

"He has?" I responded, now slightly frowning and a little concerned. But not enough to sound the alarm.

"Yeah." She assured me with a similar facial expression.

Then I came back another day to find that he'd returned again leaving a red rose. Then when I happened to be there on another shift, out of nowhere he approached the pharmacy consult window. With the creepiest grin, way too excited to see me, he leaned forward like a lead singer in an R&B group, ready with a serenade:

"Do you wanna ride in my Mercedes? There are so many things I wanna do-to-you."

He looked like Gator from *Jungle Fever*, turning my favorite Pebbles song into a perverted prose. I determined by that time he was a looney tune and that I had to leave. He can stay. I'll leave. So I did, transferring back to the one and only pharmacy I could go to. Would you believe two weeks later my husband and I were driving down a highway in Savannah only to see this guy at a stop light slowly riding by on a bike? I reclined my seat and ducked back like I was trying to avoid someone I owed money to.

"It's him! Ron, it's him!" How unlucky can one be?

******

I spent most of my days in the Low Country working in Rincon. It was a peculiar town. Split in half by the main road, Hwy 21. The alternate highway was too dangerous to take for someone who knew no one aside from her spouse. Working there was like being gifted a bitter box of dark chocolates every day. I was paid quite well there as the staff pharmacist. That region of Georgia was a part of the Charleston district in South Carolina. They paid more than the Georgia districts, allowing me to gross six-figs in my late twenties. Considering the location and culture we had to cater to there, my colleagues and I were worth every dime.

I got my first perv call while working there. It came from an unknown foreign *gentleman* with an Indian accent. Viagra was a common drug by then that most pharmacists were accustomed to dispensing daily. This apparently was his first time using it.

"I wanted to ask if I'm supposed to get this sensation," he told me in his thick accent.

"Yes. That's what it's for."

"Mmmm. Am I using it right? Uh, I'm thinking I am doing this wrong. This is ok, yes?"

"Ummm" I pause and turn to look at my tech a Puerto Rican young lady about my age. By now I'm concerned but not yet convinced.

"Ahhhhhggg... This is ok, isn't it? Ohhhhh. Is it supposed to... uhhggh? This is ok?"

In the background I hear a female groaning and sounds of what I believed to be fellatio. My mouth dropped. I looked at the phone in disbelief.

"Thank youuuu. Ahhhhggg." He hung up.

I was so taken aback. The tech who could only witness my facial expressions the whole time just peered at me with a knowing smile on her face. I had no words. Being so young, and totally caught off guard, I totally gave him the benefit of the doubt because of his foreign accent. YES, I regret it. And NO, I did not enjoy it.

******

Unrelated, years later in metro Atlanta a call would come in from someone claiming to be a customer. It had something to do with wrapping paper, fiber glass, itching, scraping brillo pad sound effects,

"cshhh, cshhh, cshhhh"

He wanted an OTC cream to resolve it. It's just as nonsensical now as it was back then. Anyway, the guy rambled on, keeping me on the phone a prolonged time. At some point the pharmacist's free advice reached its limit. I realized that I can't really help this guy but I do need to help the people right in front of me. So, I end the conversation with encouragement and wish him well. Then hung up the phone. Turns out this is a periodic phone call that rotates to different pharmacy locations. Same guy, same story, same itch. Unbeknown to him, he rotated back to me in another city. It had been a couple of years so I didn't recognize the call initially. But then the dope started making the scraping brillo sound.

"cshhh, cshhhh"

"It's you!" I said.

He chuckled having been caught and then said "goodbye." Who has time for this crap?! I called one of my Korean female colleagues who verified that she had the same encounter. We both laughed out of comradery and annoyance. I believed by then that the company has this dope to call different locations to see how we handled people who are more than reluctant to hang up when there's a ton of work and a ton of people to serve. A test of our patience and attitude. I don't know for sure to this day. But I was certainly aware of secret shoppers. If it was the case, in either case, what an asinine thing to do. There's never a boring day.

******

During one of my shifts in the Low Country, an elderly patient's husband comes in. He steps to the register but he does not have a new prescription in his hand. He seemed to be frowning so I stepped over to talk to him.

Just fyi, this is breaking protocol because we're supposed to follow workflow that keeps the pharmacist from walking over to the register or "drop-off" window. There really is no window, just a wide-open space where everybody within a 10 ft. radius can hear your business. I'm supposed to acknowledge patrons and let them stand there waiting until the technician, who works the drive-thru window and the front counter, gets finished helping at the drive-thru. If that makes sense. There's also a second technician at the filling station. But...she or he cannot cross the forbidden imaginary boundary line of the filling station. Workflow in retail is designed to optimize productivity. It's supposed to make the work flow. Except the brainiac that came up with the format forgot to factor in understaffing, rush hour, billing issues, questions from customers and the soon to come immunization station. Somewhere there is an understaffed pharmacy on the planet, Utopia, where this design works without failure. But my two techs are occupied. And there's no way I'm going to ignore this person who clearly needs my attention.

I approached the gentleman and he showed me a zip lock bag with a fentanyl patch in it. Before I could ask anything, he proceeds to inform me that his wife had passed away the day before. I immediately offer my condolences. His voice sounded as if he had been weeping. With a somber tone he continued,

"I didn't realize how strong this stuff was." He pointed at the patch in the bag. "I would have locked it away. I didn't know. I would have locked it up. I didn't know."

"I'm very sorry," I responded with sincerity. I spoke with him a few more minutes. He revealed that his wife was overusing the patches. She was placing one patch on her torso then another without removing the previous patch. I don't know how long she was doing this.

"You can take this. I don't need it. She's gone."

He handed the zip lock bag to me. I took it. But before discarding it in the hazardous waste container, I was curious about the matter and decided to look up the prescription in the computer. I saw the prescription and strength. It was on the high end but that wasn't abnormal for a terminal cancer patient. What gave me cause to pause was the directions. It read to "apply one patch every 72 hours." We typically dispense directions with the assumption that all recipients have, at the most, a 5th grade education. It is possible that an individual might interpret "apply every 72 hours" at face value. Transdermal synthetic opioids were fairly new and were not to be taken for granted. I didn't dispense the patches that way. I would include "remove patch before applying another." So, I knew I wasn't the verifying pharmacist. But I did contact the prescribing physician who wrote the prescription that was dispensed and repeated the directions as he wrote it verbatim. He was unphased saying,

"The husband probably just felt guilty because he kept giving it to her."

I told the dispensing pharmacist so that she was aware. I thought we were all cautioned to include in the directions removing the previous patch prior to applying another for fentanyl. It just seemed like we didn't do our part in terms of patient safety. The practitioners involved clearly suspected they knew better but abused the drug.

******

The busiest store in Savannah on Derenne Avenue was my thorn. I remember the mean customers. Then not having enough help and more mean customers. It affected everyone. The attitudes were infectious inside and out. It wasn't even my regular location. I would help out on occasion because they could not seem to keep a regular staffing of pharmacists. I called there once to find out if they had a particular medication that I did not have in stock while working at another location in Savannah. This was common. No big deal. The tech who picked up the phone I had become friends with. She was in a frenzy. She went on a rant about some customer, then a staff member and a manager. After that she went in,

"...you know what, I don't even care because they can have this shit! I'm sick of it! They don't even care! I don't need this! Because even when you do...."

I tilted my head forward and looked at the phone, then in the opposite direction with concern and confusion. It was a bad day. Scratch that. It was a hellacious day for her. She doesn't lose her cool. Slow to anger. And there she was on the phone yelling, losing her cool.

"What happened GiGi?"

That was all I could think of to say. I didn't really want an answer to that question. I needed an answer to the original question,

"Do you have Propranolol ER 120mg?"

"Let me check," she responded as helpful as usual.

I care about her and all those underpaid technicians. I don't ever not care. Excuse the double negative. But sometimes you have to pivot for the sake of priority. I know and feel your pain. I just can't lay your head on my double Ds at this moment.

"Yeah, we got it," she said after a successful shelf search.

"Great!" I replied with joy. "Can I give you a prescription number?"

******

Detective "Andrew" was well known among local business owners, physicians and quite naturally the local pharmacists, as this was during the height of the opioid and methamphetamine epidemic. Effingham County was affectionately known as "Methingham County." It was the lawless beast of the Low Country despite what the locals might have outsiders who move there to believe. Just as the crack cocaine era was devastating to poor Black communities, methamphetamine plagued poor White communities. Before the general public knew it, the dynamic had shifted. But not the jail time. Prison sentencing for crack possession was so long, that the epidemic of crack declined. While almost simultaneously another cheap, deadly drug arrived, almost replacing the other. The methamphetamine addiction era had successfully overshadowed the crack cocaine era. My husband and I had no idea the area we moved to was a manufacturing hub and sanctuary for methamphetamine consumers and entrepreneurs.

Detective Andrew stayed on the move. He'd show up at the beauty shop, the bank, the hospital and doctors' offices. I spotted him one time behind a gas station one evening with a few other men. I wasn't sure if he was working undercover or just getting intel from informants in an ongoing investigation. I just knew never to acknowledge him when I saw him outside of my workplace. He was always busy because there was always illegal drug activity. It was concentrated in that small town. I remember seeing the detective a lot even at restaurants. It seemed like he was always around. Or at least wherever I was there he was. He'd pop up at the pharmacy unannounced asking questions. We'd oblige within legal parameters. For instance, if he asked for a prescription hardcopy, legally we could not and did not hand it over. That request required a subpoena. But, if he or local authorities asked for the pseudoephedrine log, the magic ingredient needed to make meth that by law required a valid ID to purchase, no problem.

There were customers that were arrested but I don't think any were apprehended on store property. It would have to be at the behest of a physician whose prescription pad was stolen or signature was forged. One brazen young lady was held for less than a week for forgery and had the nerve to return to the pharmacy in red teddy bear printed pajamas and a white t-shirt the day she was released. Presumably it was the same attire she wore when handcuffed.

What stands out still to this day, are mind-blowing variations in sentencing when comparing meth to crack cocaine. Just for purposes of lesser fines and abbreviated prison terms it was more beneficial for a crack addict to switch to meth. I use the word "beneficial" cautiously. A crack addict looked like a hot mess while the other looked like a hot mess with meth mouth. They both pose the same risk to society in crime to others, and of course to themselves by inhaling either or. But one user certainly pays a higher price than the other with regard to the law.

******

A veteran officer, Rita, who frequented the pharmacy in "Methingham" County once shared with me an encounter she had during a traffic stop south of the city. Rita was good for story-telling using hand motions and a bit of a drama queen.

"I approached the vehicle, and it was a teenager, a white boy, in the driver seat with his left hand on the wheel." The other hand she hadn't noticed reaching for something else.

She could tell immediately by his expression that it wouldn't be a smooth encounter but not in a million years did she expect the response that she got from a routine traffic stop.

"I asked him for his driver's license," she motioned.

He quickly drew his right hand from over the passenger seat, she thought to get his ID. Instead, he drew a semi-automatic gun and pointed it at her face.

"Ahhh!" She screamed.

Rita freaked out and ran towards her squad car. The teen took off down the highway. In a panic, she radioed for assistance. All these sirens could be heard flooding to the same highway. Thankfully she had a thorough description of the vehicle and license plate number. The young idiot drove home. Turns out he had just picked up a few packages of Methingham's finest rocks to be delivered to his mother, the town queen pin. He thought the officer was aware of his activity. He panicked.

She told me still in a state of disbelief, "I had no idea who he was! I sho didn't know he had a gun on him!"

The panicked act by the teen escalated a simple traffic stop from a warning for speeding to multiple felony counts including weapons possession, drug trafficking and fleeing the scene during a traffic stop. Rita was so shaken up. I wasn't for certain if she returned to work after that horrible incident. What I did know for sure was that the new war on drugs was in clear view in this town but remained underreported nationally as it spread there and into numerous other Southern suburbs.

******

Of course, you cannot have a dialog about the meth epidemic and not mention its main ingredient. Sudafed (pseudoephedrine) became the pharmacist's worst nightmare. The dummies at the Three Letter Pharmacy across the street were selling it at the front counter right by the store entrance. They were fined. It was and is still illegal to sell outside of the pharmacy.

Willing accomplices were typically paid $20 to purchase as much of the product as they could in one transaction for someone higher in the chain. Usually, they'd pick a white female between her 20s and 40s, sometimes with kids in tow. She was the epitome of innocence. She would also be the front for Tussionex prescriptions, Oxycodone, Soma and Xanax. A black guy tries. A black guy is denied. A white guy maybe, maybe not. But a white girl? Send her. They'll never deny her. And for a long time, we didn't.

******

I wasn't too fond of living in Rincon, let alone having to work there. It was the cradle of where my professional and personal problems festered. Coincidently, it was where I made the most money. For the three years we lived there, out of routine I would inform my husband about my usual sucky day. It was all for not because, if you let him tell the tale of Effingham County and the Low Country back then, life was all good. I chalked it up to him being blind as a bat or whatever and never having to deal with the area's ill residents. Even today he reminisces over the penchant of his peers there for engaging in multiple sports: flag football, baseball, basketball and kickball. He loved the comradery. I, on the other hand, recount the nostalgia of an out of touch population, too many without insurance sprinkled with drug addicts dropping off fake opioid prescriptions, and daily questions of "Are you the pharmacist?." Then staring at them as they look over my shoulder to ask my white male intern questions as if *he* was the pharmacist. I recall the belligerent doctor who routinely self-prescribed Tramadol and dared us not to fill it. Or the arrogant hospital physician with a god-complex who wrote a letter of lies to my supervisor trying to get me fired because I refused to fill a prescription he wrote incorrectly. Never mind that the prescription could've and should've been taken elsewhere since he was too arrogant to correct it. He and his position were beyond reproof and how dare I inform him of his error. And of course, there was the occasional false accusation by a handful of patients claiming they were "missing" Percocet, Gabapentin, Xanax or Vicodin tablets. All of which are double counted by the pharmacist after it's counted by the technician under surveillance. They're never missing blood pressure tablets or diabetic pills, or three tablets short of a full cholesterol prescription—nope, just the good stuff.

Overall, the impression Effingham County left on me was this:

1) No one should leave the pharmacy counter without being counseled on how to use new, potentially dangerous medication.

2) The so-called war on drugs as it pertained to the opioid epidemic and methamphetamine was heavily underreported in White suburbia, and

3) Those people hated, hated President Obama.

A couple of pharmacies I frequented in another county enacted the "count it yourself" rule for certain repeat accusers. When they came to pick up their goodie bag of happy pills, we'd have them recount the recounted tablets in their bottle using our spatula and counting tray while we were standing in front of them across the counter at the consultation window. I know it seems ludicrous and unnecessary. But I'm telling you we had to. People were that deceptive.

******

It was a joyous day when we finally departed Effingham Co., Ga. Three years my husband suffered me and the kids. My son by then had been brain washed by his teachers in believing Sarah Palin was a favorable candidate for VP (straight face emoji). My husband's company escorted us out of there three times faster than it took for us to move there. They packed up our home. We packed up our kids. I've blocked out much of the nonsensical encounters in that part of the state. It's a coping mechanism. It also helps to not look back. Even though I clearly did.

15

"Generic Sudafed Please?"

Picking up shifts on either border of the state of Georgia was always a risk. You were highly likely to encounter a high volume of Oxycodone prescriptions, a high volume of pseudoephedrine purchases, and an equally high volume of looniness. Bremen, Ga was one of those western border rural areas around 2012 where you were guaranteed to encounter all of those characters on any given day. As much as I tried to avoid picking up a shift in that town it proved to be impossible because it was well within my radius. I lived in Villa Rica; Bremen's I 20 neighbor. The first time I visited was a blur. But all subsequent shifts I can only wish were deleted from my memory.

I happened to meet one of the many pharmacy managers there (that never lasted at that location) when I strolled in for an afternoon shift that day, covering for his staff pharmacist. He was a tall white male, a respectable looking guy with a typical right-side part hairstyle. I spoke then took my place beside the consult window, signed on to the computer and got to work. Not long after, while the tech was busy at the drive-

213

thru, a couple of customers stepped up to the counter so I immediately step over to assist them. The first was a middle-aged individual, wearing a black button-down western-style shirt, with his hands half-way in his pockets who looked like he could be a twin of the Marlboro Man. He was pleasant until he wasn't. Long story short, he was there because his prescription eye drops were not filled with the rest of his meds that he picked up over a week ago. He did not take that too well, mainly because he lived a distance away and hated making multiple trips to the pharmacy. He said begrudgingly,

"I told y'all about it before and it keeps happening!"

'So why does it keep happening?' I'm thinking to myself. "I'm sorry about that. I'll take a look at your profile to see what's going on."

I check his prescription profile. Scrolling through his list of meds, I see it. To my surprise, I quickly found the issue. The day supply didn't coincide with his other maintenance meds. The problem could be fixed by increasing the day supply of the eyedrops from 25 to 30. But I don't tell him that believing that information would only piss him off. While the not-so-helpful manager gets his eyedrops ready I apologize again for an inconvenient oversight that had nothing to do with me. But I'm there at that moment, so... He's not interested in another *I'm sorry.*

"I don't want another apology. I want it fixed!"

Understood. I fixed it. Then I stall until I get the prescription in hand and assured him in the manager's presence,

"Your eyedrops are aligned with your other maintenance

214

meds. You won't have this problem again. I've also flagged your profile as an alert to fill those drops with your other meds."

He seemed satisfied flashing that Marlboro Man grin at me. Except that he said something like,

"It better *not* happen again," while still grinning and simultaneously raising his shirt to flash a pistol under it.

******

That location's first customers of the day were guaranteed to be pseudoephedrine purchasers. Not one, not two or three, but all of them. Whether there were five people in line or nine people in line, they ALL wanted the same thing. It was around that time that those customers got smart and realized they didn't have to ask for generic Sudafed. The requests were varied, "generic Claritin D," or "Alavert D." But the usual was generic Sudafed. It cost the least for the most of the essential ingredient. It was the most tolerated transactional abuse of OTC medication. Pharmacists reported the trend for years. As far as the large pharmacy chains were concerned, particularly the one I worked for at the time, the plea for intervention fell on deaf ears for a long time. Pharmacists saw the misuse. Corporate saw the revenue. Their response blind or not was to not support efforts to inhibit our part in an epidemic, but to bolster supply for a long time to meet the demand.

So how then do pharmacy staff members respond when the ethical responsibility as it was, began and ended with us. Well, we either refuse the sale or we sell, sell, sell.

Pharmacists were burdened with a conscience that skated down the middle. The ununified decision was to not punish the innocent for the crimes of the guilty. But who's innocent and who's guilty? Are we supposed to size people up at the counter and determine who actually suffered from sinus congestion and who was just at stop number 2 of 3 to stockpile and distribute? I don't know what the rest did. But here's what I did. I listened to the staff. If a tech informs me that a customer comes in routinely to get the same thing (i.e., Bronkaid, Primatene Mist spray, generic Sudafed, etc.) and the staff pharmacist routinely approves or rejects the sale, then so do I. Remember, I'm the visiting floater. I don't rock the boat. But if I happen to be staff during that particular phase, I monitor behavior and routine. If you get prescriptions with us, you can purchase pseudoephedrine. If you visit sparingly, you can purchase pseudoephedrine. If you appear nervous, in a hurry, rude, or approached the counter out of the blue and/or do not fill prescriptions with us, you cannot purchase pseudoephedrine. That was that, until I visited Bremen.

What I learned was that "buyers" or "stockpilers" came in all kinds of creative forms. There's the businessman, the young single mother with kids, the middle-aged single mother with kids, the grandma, the grandpa, the guy on the cellphone having an important imaginary business conversation pretending to not be able to find what he's looking for. And my favorite, the *"I'm going to tell management if you don't sell this drug to me,"* buyer.

What was most indicative was the time of day they rolled in off the street. The Bremen buyers want to beat the crowd. They rush in first thing in the morning at 8 a.m. right behind the morning pharmacist just unlocking the door and raising the shutters to begin their day. It's enough to spook you if you didn't already know why they were following you. So, this particular morning, I'd had enough. I didn't want to be in Bremen let alone deal with the buyers' club that morning. So, guess what? Nobody's getting what they want. *They gonna learn today!*

I raise the shutters and 4 or 5 people are standing in a single line.

"Good morning!" I chimed.

"Can I get generic Sudafed?"

"No."

"Why not?"

"I'm not selling any this morning." He walks away. Number 2 walks up.

"Sudafed please?"

"No."

"It's right there. You're not going to sell it to me?"

"Not today!" I reaffirmed. He storms off. Another buyer walks up to the end of the line. Buyer #3 steps up,

"Generic Sudafed."

"I can't sell it to you." He lingers. Up steps #4.

I didn't get a chance to reject #4. The store manager approached the pharmacy with a disgruntled customer. It was #2. Mr. Pope, the manager, tapped in the pharmacy door code and walked through to approach me.

"Why aren't you selling the Sudafed?"

What I wanted to say was that I didn't have to, company policy says so. But what I think I said was,

"I believe that it was being abused and I did not feel comfortable being a part of the problem today."

"Well, what if management sold it instead?" Mr. Pope suggested. "Just page one of us and we'll come to the pharmacy."

"Ok," I responded while walking back to my verification station.

You asked for it, I was thinking. It's about 8:05 A.M.

Mr. Pope completed the remaining transactions while in the pharmacy. Everyone wanted a pseudoephedrine product. Everyone got a pseudoephedrine product. Once done, Mr. Pope walked out just as calm as he walked in and returned to his morning duties.

I resumed my morning solo routine and looked up at the clock hanging on the wall to the right above my work station. It's about ten after eight. Five, four, three, two… one. I acknowledge the customer.

"Good morning. How may I help you?"

"Can I get generic Sudafed please?" I pick up the phone to page for help as suggested.

"I need a manager to the pharmacy for customer assistance please."

I expect to see Mr. Pope returning. What I got was an assistant manager instead. He was a six- feet plus, tall guy on the heavy side. He wore the usual managerial attire: a long sleeve button down white shirt and a tie, gray vest with a name tag and black pants like Mr. Pope. He tapped in the pharmacy code and entered the pharmacy.

"He wants Sudafed," I told my helper. Another buyer walks up.

This is what I go through before an hour of filling prescriptions has gone by. I'm standing there as a gatekeeper fighting a battle I have no chance of winning because people who should be my allies (management and corporate) are my enemies in that they choose to turn a blind eye towards a major problem they have no interest in being held accountable for.

******

Prior to the P2P version of methamphetamine, the epidemic wasn't nearly as intricate as the crack cocaine epidemic. It was much easier to track and all but eliminate. When it comes to domestic transactions there's an easily accessible source that bolsters the production of meth. Consider the scenario where you, the illegitimate consumer, have to get product from me a legal gatekeeper working within a legal supplier. I or some other employee in the supply chain would have to be willing to ignore ethics to continuously order pseudoephedrine to keep up with its current demand. Then look the other way while selling the product, let's say weekly, to you. The response from management at this particular pharmacy is a quintessential example of how the ethical violation occurs. If I, the gatekeeper, decide to refuse to sell pseudoephedrine out of suspicion of it being abused, I would get overruled by the knowledgeable, yet unethical overseer who pretends NOT to see.

My opinion about the war on drugs in the U.S. is that it has never been unwinnable. It's been unwilling. It takes more than action from the police. Civilians play a larger role than what we're held accountable for. It takes a *good guy* to facilitate the process, in this case, of supplying a legal product that ultimately gets converted into an illegal product, for illegal distribution and use.

Pseudoephedrine is to meth what retail pharmacy corporations are to cookers of meth. There's a legal entity indirectly connected to the illegal entity that drives the business. The corporate heads and even the retail management and willing pharmacists believe or want to believe their hands are clean in the matter (because it's perfectly legal to sell pseudoephedrine). And God forbid they piss off a customer by refusing to sell the stuff and ultimately get into trouble with customer service representatives. In actuality, our hands are ALL dirty, filthy as a meth addict. I'll add that they are dirtier because for the longest time, many of us looked the other way by choosing peace and profit over people. But then more and more pharmacists became fed up without having the backing of the companies we worked for.. That made us powerless. So then how do you get the overseers to change? By hitting them where it hurts the most—their bottom line. At least two of the top 3 pharmacy retailers were fined tens of millions of dollars by the feds for their role in the methamphetamine and opioid epidemic. One of the company's owned a distribution center that was shut down in addition to the fines. It didn't eradicate the problem but it certainly forced retailers to implement policy restrictions that finally backed the pharmacists' right to deny sales.

******

Here in Bremen, the assistant manager grabs the 96-count of generic Sudafed as another buyer requested, and completes the transaction. He then leaves the pharmacy. Then disappeared down one of the aisles of overpriced items to return to do whatever the assistant manager does at 8:18 a.m. Another customer walks up to the pharmacy counter. I greet him.

"Hello! How can I help you?"

"Can I get generic Sudafed?"

I reach for the nearest phone to page,

"Customer assistance needed in the pharmacy please."

I go back to my morning biz in hopes that I can complete prescription #1 before 9am. It's 8:19. Three more patrons walk up and stand in line. One is a middle age-looking white lady holding her purse under her arm. She looks anxious but not in an annoying way. She just leaned to the right while gripping that purse. The guy behind her I can already see is going to be a problem. The assistant manager returns. He sees a brand-new line of early bird pill peddling patrons. He walks around the line, taps the code to the pharmacy security door, heads to the register to oblige each one.

"How can I help you?" He said.

"I need the 96-count generic Sudafed."

The assistant manager reaches for it.

"You're not using this for something illegal, are you?" He asked the guy before scanning the item.

"Oh no sir! No! I need it."

"Well... ok. 'cause we don't want to have a problem here."

"No sir. There's no problem."

The assistant manager completes the transaction and helps the next buyer.

No sooner did my face reveal a condescending smirk in his direction did the man child standing behind the anxious lady slam an Alavert-D card on the patient consult counter right by me and demand that he be sold the product immediately. I remained calm with my hands still on the keyboard not having quite resolved an insurance rejection for prescription #1. I looked up at the man child wearing a white polo shirt and floral shorts. He had items in his left hand and his right hand still on the card he slammed on the counter.

"Sir we only have one register this morning you'll have to wait in line," I informed him unphased by his childlike behavior.

He yelled something unmemorable like a kid who was just
told he couldn't have a sugar-coated cereal. I proceeded to
type and resolve the insurance issue for prescription #1. He
picked up the Alavert-D card and got his ass back in line. The
anxious lady gripping her purse who was waiting just the
same as the man child and others, was in front of him
chuckling at the guy as he walked by like she had witnessed a
rookie in the morning buy. *Keep your mouth shut. Wait in
line. Get the product. Get out,* I imagined she was thinking.

The early bird pseudoephedrine transactions ended at
approximately 8:44 A.M.

16

Mortar and Pestle

I believe it's typical for most women to put ourselves last trying to be all things to all those around us. Our marriage, kids, career, other relationships, so on and so forth. Everyone and everything else come before our own needs. But we have to turn that around. If I had any regret at all it would be self-neglect. Only in recent years have women been encouraged to put ourselves, our own well-being first. It's proudly referred to as "self-care" these days. Prior to this announcement I'm pretty sure women of my generation and those who are older sought refuge in an individual choice of antidepressants, church, alcohol, Oprah and/or Judge Judy. I've only been a female all my life and I still cannot explain the propensity to internalize a sense of guilt that accompanies *putting my mask on first.*

When flying we are told a thousand times in case of an emergency if the plane loses cabin air pressure to *"put your mask on first,"* then your child's. It's common sense. But somehow our brains are wired to save and protect those we love, even at our own peril. What a burden to bear. Self-care is essential whether you live alone or support a 3-generation home. Our mental and physical well-being matter. How we feel on the job and about our jobs matter. Our home life matters.

I *could not* seem to find a balance between prioritizing myself, work and family early on in my career. While working full-time, nurturing the hubby and kids, I was watching everyone but me enjoy my home and the life I helped build. Alternatively, when ambition took over, where I focused on my own entrepreneurial endeavors and work, I managed to neglect my family. I was either too tired or too distracted.

In 2008, we moved to the aforementioned Rincon, GA, a town too far from Atlanta and too close to right-wing infused regression. However, I definitely appreciated the above average compensation while working there. I was the staff pharmacist at the only W Pharmacy in town. That lasted about a year or so. I eventually floated to locations in nearby cities like Savannah, Garden City, and Wilmington Island. Eventually, though, I'd swing back around to Rincon. I was all about work and reward at that time. I even had the audacity to open a small business just because I was my father's child. My dad owned a self-serve laundromat for over 20 years and typically had multiple sources of income. So, I figured it was natural for me to do the same. I owned an infant and toddler clothing boutique named *Little Bo-Tique*, about two miles from where I lived. I managed the business during the week and worked there on the weekends that I was not scheduled at the pharmacy. Owning a business in my mind is what I was supposed to do. It was a short-term goal. Something else I wanted to own. It also gave me a reason to not be present at home. Before I realized it, my spouse and kids took a backseat to what I wanted at the time. I also managed rental property which required me to travel from time to time when communicating via email became insufficient. By insufficient I mean tenants not responding to emails or phone calls inquiring as to why the rent wasn't paid on time or at all. Travel also included visiting my family 12 and 14 hours away from Rincon when I could.

But as it is impossible to have it all, I came to realize at some point that my position within the household had shifted right before my eyes. It hit me on the day that my 3-year-old daughter, Nailah, sitting in a high chair was so unabashed in telling me, after I turned the tv off at dinner time,

"This is daddy's house."

"What did you say?" I asked her returning to the dinner table.

"This is daddy's house. And that's daddy's tv," as if she was talking to another three-year-old who just committed an offense instead of her own mother.

"This is my house! That's my tv! Your daddy didn't pay for ....!"

For a moment I could've morphed into Jennifer Anniston's character on *The Morning Show* when speaking to her ungrateful daughter in that dormitory scene. But of course, I said none of that to my little precious miseducated daughter. She's only 3. I was stunned nonetheless.

The next bout with my unfiltered Mini-me was again at the dinner table, legs swinging in the high chair, where she

informed me that my mother was no longer *Grandmamma*.
She's *Grandma* now. Her daddy's mom was *Grandmamma*. I
pierced over at Ron at a safe distance on the opposite end of
the table. He didn't even look my way. Ron just grinned
deceitfully at our impressionable daughter. He knew what I
was thinking without making eye contact,

"I can't believe you did that." My piercing eyes daring him to
look my way.

Who was I to this family right now? Not to make a mountain
out of a molehill, but a mother and wife would understand
what transpired in my absence. Paternal manipulation.
"Grandmamma" by default sounds more affectionate than
"Grandma." "Grandma" is the other grandmother. *I* didn't tell
the kids to call my mother that. They just did. Now this aura
of who they should be closer to is planted in their minds. No
words were exchanged for the rest of that evening. At least
not from me.

My son, Malcolm, was six by that time. He was a good big
brother taking time to play with his little sister daily. But as a
unit, the kids had become terribly unruly at home,
particularly with me. They had developed this order of
command that determined when to obey and when to disobey.
This is where if daddy said to do something they'd better do
it. If daddy said "stop" they'd better stop. But if mommy said
"stop," well, they would collectively decide, *we'll just press
our luck and keep at our antics. Mommy will get distracted
and forget that we were up to no good. She's too busy.* It was
true.

One hilarious yet annoying afternoon I was looking for yet

another item that I thought I'd placed in its usual spot but couldn't find it. I'm either progressively absent-minded or my children are domestic bandits. One day it would be my earrings. Another day it may be my shoes or my favorite pen that my three-year-old used to write her name on the wall just outside my bedroom like some not-so-bright graffiti artist. This particular day it was my smartphone. An interrogation of the usual guilty suspects ensues.

"Have either of you seen my cell phone?"

"No, mommy." Both replied, looking up at me clueless.

They then resumed their usual routine of play. Neither of them knows where it is. I continue searching. Then a couple of hours later it magically reappears in the family room on the couch. I know I checked the couch. Ordering new inventory and filing taxes are on my mind at this point so it never occurs to me to re-interrogate the suspects as to how it got to a spot where I knew I had searched and how I knew they had it in the first place. I just didn't know *why* they had it. Well, I found out nearly a year later right before we moved. I just so happen to be looking for stored pictures on my phone when I noticed footage that I did not remember recording. I pressed play. The two little stooges were filming each other on my smartphone, singing and dancing. Nothing wrong with that. But then my daughter could be seen mocking and teasing who or whatever, probably me. She put her thumbs in her ears waving her hands back and forth while sticking her tongue out.

"Neh, neh, ni, neh, neh! Neh, neh ni, neh, neh!"

She mocked in between making some blubber noises. Then while continuing to dance, jumping up and down, she turned around and pulled her pants down to moon the camera. Her brother who was filming the whole thing could be heard laughing hysterically while his little sister played percussion on her behind. Just as I took a deep inhale to yell their names telling them to "Come here right now!" I burst into laughter. I could not believe…why? Just why? And the nerve to do so with my phone! Then never to delete the evidence! Zero regard for maternal consequence. They would have never had the nerve to do this with their father's phone. As humorous as that infamous video was, by then, the writing was on the wall. Looking back, my children had developed a level of disregard for maternal authority. I knew it would only get worse as they got older if I didn't intervene. Overall, I blamed myself. I wasn't there. At times, even when I was there, I wasn't there. Reality set in. *This isn't working.* When a woman chooses love, that is marriage and/or children, her life is no longer hers. I can never put myself first.

✶✶✶✶✶✶

"Volatile" is the word my husband used to describe that phase when I was all work; no wife. *Insignificant* is how I described the way he treated me. *Emasculating* is how I treated him. *Disjointed* is what we both were.

We had it good and had it difficult at the same time. There was a power struggle at home. We were both playing a role in the conflict. It was as if our careers and placement within the household could not co-exist. Without realizing it at that time I was treating my husband like a subordinate. What I wanted and needed superseded anything he may have wanted or needed. In my mind I'd done and was doing more than enough. All I saw were the sacrifices I made to get us to where we were and what I was doing to keep it all together.

******

We'd moved to the first of many towns where nobody knew who we were when we landed in Rincon. I was able to get a full-time job before setting foot in that town. I saw in my opinion the worst that town had to offer on a regular basis while my husband experienced the complete opposite. Not a week went by where I wasn't playing defense against a substance abuser, a willfully ignorant racist native of the community, or a dismissive individual presumably because I looked too young to be a pharmacist. My guard was always up. It was exhausting and it was miserable. But I do what *we* do, persevere. I was paying for daycare, a car, and two mortgages until we could rent our first home since we couldn't sell it.

That time marked the beginning of what became a nation-wide housing crisis coupled with the unveiling of a great portion of America's deep-seated hatred as the first African American President took office. It's an unexplained anomaly to be so loved and so hated at the same time. But that was the atmosphere especially at that time, in that town, in this country.

But let me reel this back in. Whatever was needed of me, whenever, I gave it. At home, at work, I am giving. Any working woman, wife and/or mom can relate. *We are relentless givers.* We make sacrifices to a fault. All the while my young and athletic hubby had plenty of time for parks and recreation, joining whatever seasonal sport he could plug himself into. Not to mention he had a passion for video games that I will never understand. I resented him for not realizing all that I'd done for his comfort and career.

There were moments where we just could not see I to eye. I wanted him to pay more attention to his dismissive kids, how they responded (or didn't respond) to their mother. Be more attentive to the home. Literally, notice when things are not functioning properly with the new house we'd just built. Whether it was the exhaust fan being worn out from leaving it on throughout the night, or the "new" microwave malfunctioning. Being home when a repair man came to repair the "new" microwave. Be there when the cable guy finally shows up between the hours of 8 A.M. and 10 P.M. Be the one who gets pissed off because the cable guy shows up 10 minutes before your shift so you have to tell the guy, "Get lost. I've been waiting all day. I gotta get to work." Ron wanted me to stop complaining about what he wasn't doing because he believed he was doing his best. He's never been married before (neither have I). And although this was the second house we built, we didn't live in the first one long enough to adjust to the responsibility of the upkeep. Some things I believe a man should know instinctively, like how to fix everything. My father fixed everything. Ron believed I should know how to cook everything. His mother cooked everything. "Jesus... we have a problem."

There was no winning, only built-up adversity. We were co-dependent roommates prioritizing work, kids and other people over our marriage. Swing shifts are required for my line of work. So, I wouldn't be home in the evenings on many occasions. When I do get home it's around 10:30pm. There was no time for "how was your day," "did the kids do their homework," "was there enough leftovers," etc. It was, get home, say "hello," maybe eat late, maybe not, take a shower. Get over whatever kind of sucky evening at work I might have had before getting into bed, so that I can get some decent sleep. Get up. Get ready. Get the kids ready. Get them to school. Get to work. Get the AM version of whatever happened in the PM the evening before.

I didn't ask or complain about anything that Ron cooked when I couldn't. He was the King of Hamburger Helper. Although at some point during our tug-of-war, I must have mouthed off too much about something. I came home exhausted one night after working the evening shift. All the lights were off downstairs and nothing was left on the stove for me to eat. No Hamburger Helper Beef Stroganoff. No Hamburger Helper Beef and Macaroni. No green beans. Nothing. I get upstairs and Ron was all tucked in and turned over on his side of the bed facing the window as to not see my face if he happened to be awake when I came home. I didn't even have the energy to pick up where I left off, let alone start a new argument over the obvious intentional omission of no food being left out for me. Such a nonverbal way to say "Take that!" By that time, if we were taking score in this "who's feeling most unappreciated" battle, Ron was winning.

Looking back, we were both unappreciative and inattentive to one another. That convoluted view allowed him to be oblivious to me being disrespected as a professional, as his wife and mother of his children. Someone could literally say something out of line to me, friend or family, and he'd say nothing. Ron's a non-confrontational kind of guy, much like my older brothers. The residual effect was that his protection was nowhere to be found. No wife wants to feel unprotected. So, my tenacity and this proverbial brick wall I built around myself took its place. He made no visible room for understanding. I in return defaulted to wearing the pants and the skirt in the home emasculating my equal. Our lop-sided income back then didn't help either. That only bolstered my bad attitude. Soon after I began to wonder if I had become that educated absent wife that became intolerable to her spouse to the point where he resented her success. Something had to give.

******

Ron and I weren't communicating at some point for almost a week. I cannot remember what ignited the mutual silent treatment. Probably another *'you don't appreciate me'* argument. I had a day off in the middle of the week. Taking advantage of an empty house, I decided to clean up. I went to dump the trash and found maggots in our garbage receptacle. There were a lot of them. The big flies that birthed them were there but scattered upon my arrival. The container was being kept in the garage. I knew it was a bad idea when it started to smell. But I didn't move it outside. Neither did Ron. I gagged when I saw the maggots swarming over liquid that came from leftover whatever from days ago at the bottom of the receptacle. I just refused to tend to this on my own. I sent Ron a text while he was at work. I would've called giving him the gory details of what I discovered except we weren't speaking to each other. He later came home. Before coming inside, he cleaned out the receptacle with a water hose. He washed away the remnant left on the garage floor until there was no sign or smell of what had been lurking right under our noses. Then he set the receptacle outside at the back of the house where it couldn't be seen from the street. Where we should've put it in the first place. He then came in. I'm sure I thanked him. He went to scrub his hands with soap and water in the guest bath that I'd used to scrub my hands. I'd finished cooking by the time he came in. I'm sure he appreciated me for having dinner ready at a reasonable hungry hour after work. I made meatloaf, garlic butter mashed potatoes and green beans. He loved meatloaf. We sat at the table together to eat dinner. Neither of us blamed the other for the disgusting mess that had festered in the receptacle. No argument over who's dumb idea it was to place it in the garage. We ate dinner peacefully then methodically resumed verbal communication that evening.

******

Unfortunately, bad times in our marriage didn't end there. The breaking point came when I arrived home dead tired one night thinking about nothing but the nap I needed before I had to return to the hell hole the next morning. I'd just walked in the bedroom and took one shoe off.

My husband needed something from me and I refused to give it to him citing something so absurd to this day I cannot believe those words came out of my mouth. He was looking at me in a state of shock or maybe like he was being addressed by a stranger in his bedroom. Mentally and physically exhausted, I had nothing left that night. I plopped onto my side of the bed trying to take the other shoe off my aching feet. All I could gather after a long, overwhelming shift was, '*here was another needy person wanting something else from me that I am now too exhausted to give*' and I didn't give a damn about hurting their feelings. Regretfully, that someone was my husband. He expressed his displeasure the next morning probably after thinking through the night to digest what his wife had the nerve to say to him.

"What you said to me last night," he recounted. "I'm not going to be spoken to like that."

He sat at the edge of the bed, not quite making eye contact, clasping his hands. He would have otherwise already been dressed for work.

"You are not going to disrespect me."

It could have been the fatigue. I was looking for a scapegoat.

"I'm sorry. It's the pills I switched to. It..."

I blamed my mindless response on the birth control pills I was taking at the time. It was a tricyclic prescription that sent my emotions on a rollercoaster ride. He wasn't hearing it, cutting me off.

"I don't care! I am not going to be spoken to that way."

I heard him loud and clear. I hadn't seen that look he gave me since college when I was super late returning his car that he allowed me to borrow for a day. I needed to admit to myself that I wasn't being a good wife. And I needed him to realize what it meant to be a better husband to a working wife.

A few years later we were settling into our first dream home. While unpacking I examined my second of three wedding rings and a paper cut on the same finger. I came to the

conclusion that Ron had an affair at some point during our marriage. I eventually accused him to his face. I'd convinced myself that I knew just when and why, even believing that it was justified because of how I had been in the past. For that reason, real or imagined, I insisted on ring #3 believing that the upgraded ring #2 was a mere apology for having affair #1.

PART IV: REVELATION AND TRANSFORMATION

17

Mortar and Pestle (The Remix)

I wasn't happy with where our marriage was. I wasn't happy
with work and motherhood because I helped construct it that
way. I had a hand in making myself miserable. So, I turned it
around. *We* turned it around. Ron and I became each other's
advocate after moving back to the future near Atlanta in 2011
and leaving the perils of Rincon behind. I gladly put my
desires and ambitions on the shelf. They didn't seem
important anymore. I had to put him and the kids first. Be
present from now on. I supported his never-ending quest for
career advancement which meant moving many times. Which
meant reacclimating ourselves and our kids to the next town
for years. Find a house in a good neighborhood. Find good
doctors and dentists. Find good schools; get registered. Find
extracurricular for the kids. Find a job, find a church, find
peace of mind. He in return supported my need to orchestrate
some sort of balance for my work-home life.

I didn't need to follow anyone else's blueprint of what a woman (who I am first and foremost), wife and mom should be doing. I became realistic about what I could and could not handle. I decided to sacrifice my career for part-time employment in favor of my husband's career while managing the home, the kids and their activities. I managed rental properties, oversaw other investments, and obtained a master's degree online. That took 4 years. It all worked. I was home more. I was present.

The most difficult part turned out to be our kids having to forge new friendships so many times. Nailah was much better at it than Malcolm. I became quite lenient with our son as he got older believing I owed him because we snatched him away from every friend he had fought so hard to make.

******

We couldn't understand why making friends was such a task for our son. He grew from being combative as a toddler, to clingy in kindergarten to awkward in middle school around his peers. He grew disengaged. I noticed that he couldn't or wouldn't even look at me while talking to me. When he did look at me in response to whatever question I might have asked, his big, dark-brown eyes that were already wide grew wider as if he was agitated by the inquiry. He became inattentive and at a loss for words sometimes. At some point my son seemed to become detached from reality and resorted to fitting in to the reality of someone at school or some character on tv just to fit in. It took six years for me to seek professional intervention. We found out that his behavior was a pattern of mild autism. I felt like we had failed Malcolm as parents. A mother knows when something's wrong and I did. I just couldn't put my finger on it. It was Asperger's syndrome now categorized as a symptom of ASD (autism spectrum disorder). It's a form of autism easily overlooked and often misunderstood. I would have responded so differently towards his behavior had I known sooner. As a result of getting professional help our relationship is much more substantive now. I have mixed emotions over how Malcolm has managed over the years all things considered. There had to be moments where he needed our protection but only received our criticism. I asked him around the time he turned 18 how he felt about his childhood. He said it was good. I believe he forgave without saying "I forgive you." But I have yet to reconcile. I can't help but to think back on those parent-teacher meetings, incidences at school and just missing those important queues. Making the first 15 years of his life so hard has been one of my few regrets.

******

It took a while to register that marriage is a process not a power struggle. It is a giving, a receiving and a sacrifice. It is joined. It is space, as in I have my wing of the house and Ron has his (wink-n-kiss emoji). I stay out of his man cave (most of the time) when he's gaming. That allows me to be alone with my thoughts in our bedroom, aka my bedroom, that is also my sanctuary. He shows his appreciation for me these days and gives me the space I need to be my unique self.

Marriage is room for flaws and forgiveness. I forgave him. He forgave me. Forgiveness is given as many times as it is needed. We love each other now more than we did when we said "I do." We love date nights and make time for mini excursions like we did when we dated in college. We created a co-sanctuary where we can talk to each other without the influence of the outside world, family or friends. I'm intrigued by his socio-political knowledge. I still love his wit. He has such a way with words. I may have stolen a few for this memoir and social media. I still laugh at his corny jokes and laugh at how he laughs after making those corny jokes.

We enjoy each other's company and anticipate it at the end of a work day. But I cannot overstate the benefit of uninterrupted, nonjudgmental space. I even send the kids a "DND" notice via text on occasion. This is when I get to be invisible, not having to worry about anyone else's needs. I especially love disappearing during 'Jesus time.' That's when I submerge all of myself into biblical reading and research.

******

I was called into the ministry several years ago. I didn't accept until two years later (angel face emoji). Many teachers and preachers can attest that there's plenty of reasons to hesitate. Some people reject it all together. It's a life-long privilege not to be taken lightly. I didn't think I had enough sense. Why does God pick odd-ball people? But I prayed for affirmation and received it. I also fasted and prayed before writing and delivering my first sermon. Don't fret over the few choice words seasoned sparingly in this non-fictional tale of confession. I said I'm a minister. Not Jesus. Peppered with flaws. It's necessary to be authentic and true-to-form. Particularly with my proclivities. I was a cussing Christian and judgmental. Mostly rehabilitated. Being perfected, yet never perfect in this lifetime. I will never be a Bible-thumping, holy roller playing the hypocrite pretending to have it all together. The older I get the more I understand that we walk a curvy path into the Kingdom learning along the way. Like marriage, spiritual maturity is a process that begs grace and mercy. That's the soothing part of ministering, by the way—meeting people where they are without judgment. I've been preaching that message to church folk for years now.

Ministry has been my biggest and best endeavor yet. It's afforded me a sought-after contentment that my career as a pharmacist never met. It's also been my brokest as my most lucrative career wanes and the ministry waxes. But then again, since when did a person have to succeed in one thing? I can certainly do both and be my best at both.

I decided I needed a formal education in ministry. Some can jump right into the fold. The rest of us need structural training. It did cost my household financially, though. Can you imagine relinquishing a 6-figure career? But it was worth it. I didn't know half as much as I do now after obtaining a Master's in Ministry. I love it enough to do it even without compensation. Thankfully, though, like many other women I've discovered multiple ways to make income outside of my original profession as it gradually vaporizes. Diversifying my income has been rewarding. Ministering has been a labor of love with bumps and bruises, particularly while fighting church folk. But I submit to continuous efforts through faith and works learning from my mistakes along the way. I love working for Jesus. The love and grace He gives, no one can take that away. He's the best boss in the world. Any reward obtained is icing on the cake. But it does get difficult. I began praying more for guidance as a result.

Then one day my "Ah hah!" moment came while watching an old interview of Dr. Charles Stanley. I heard him say something that taught me a valuable lesson. That is to keep in mind that no matter what, to "do what God wants you to do and leave the consequences to Him."

******

Coupled compromise has also been rewarding. Ron and I are older and wiser. We are way past early marriage blues. We don't even argue and rarely get angry with one another. Mostly because we just don't have the energy anymore. We used all that up in the early years. The kids take half the blame. Worst case scenario we stop talking and get out of each other's faces for a few hours. Or we harness the anger and use it against the kids when they're goofing off, acting full grown or think the chores can do themselves.

These days we leave the marriage drama to reality tv, watching *Love & Marriage Huntsville* on the OWN network. I love my husband. He loves me. He and I are teammates with a mutual respect for one another. We listen to each other. We might even listen to the kids when they make sense. We understand and embrace the mechanism of love and marriage so much better now. Mortar and pestle—that's us. I can't do my husband's job. He can't do mine. We can exist alone but we are so much more productive, a force, when we work together.

18

Nature vs. Nurture

A technician I met several years ago while working in Union City, GA informed me that she wanted to become a pharmacist and was excited about the journey. She was particularly drawn to the salaries. For many years there was a pharmacist shortage nationwide. Remedied by this unprecedented influx of pharmacy programs that included satellite locations where students subscribed to partial remote learning. Such a thing was unheard of back in the day. I could not wrap my mind around that type of clinical learning environment. It made no sense to me. 'Pop up' pharmacy schools, was how some of us used to refer to it. It was the result of the best kept secret getting out. That a 20 something year old could not only be declared a "doctor" but also leap from a college campus ready or not into a career with the promise of a six-figure salary and $15,000 or more for a two-year contract plus an allocation to relocate. All before receiving a diploma in hand. Not to mention, pharmacy corporation reps flocked to campuses, like Xavier, and nearby venues to recruit P4 students.

That was then. Fast forward 10 years later. No sign-on. Goodbye to bonuses. Goodbye to stock options. So long to raises that were once 6% annually diminishing to 3%, then 1% then 50 cents. The technician asked if I thought problems would worsen within the profession including pharmacists' salaries being negatively affected by the current surge of pharmacy majors and expensive pharmacy schools.

"Of course, it will! Notwithstanding that the supply now outweighs the demand, motives matter. Too many recruits treat patient care and the profession secondary to money and prestige. Because of that you'll fall prey to the greedy academic institutions that are overcharging you. You'll also fall prey to your own greed, wanting the means to finance a luxury lifestyle that you actually cannot afford because of the $200,000 in student loans you'll owe that you'll never pay off because of that luxury lifestyle. Meanwhile, you'll have to work your but off in an absurd, ridiculously stressful environment whether you like it or not with no relief, nor reward, no chance of career advancement. By then retail will have worn your ass out by the time you're 36. Then you'll get desperate and job-hop in constant search of that elusive 9 to 5, no weekend job that actually doesn't pay nearly enough. Then you'll wonder why you spent so much time and money to receive so little satisfaction in return by choosing this profession in the first place. Then you'll wallow in regret. Yes, it's a problem dumb ass!"

Until recently, I don't recall ever being asked about the patients we serve. The questions are almost always self-centered. I didn't give that tech the naked truth of consequences from selfish ambition vs. service to others. Neither did I warn her about the nightmare of owing student loans and the trap of retail pharmacy. Instead, I offered encouragement in effort to avoid crushing the life out of her gold-plated endeavor.

"Nah, you'll be fine."

******

I'll never forget the ultrasound images of my daughter, Nailah, sucking her thumb. A few hours after being born she appeared deep in thought, exploring her surroundings or perhaps she was judging them. My husband and I avoided learning her gender, mainly because we just knew she was going to be a boy. The coin on my hubby's side of the family was testosterone dominant. I didn't want to get my hopes up. So, when that little 6lb,10oz bundle of joy made her entrée, my husband and I high-fived each other like we won a state championship game. My mother was present. I was glad she was there. That is until she inserted her unsolicited remarks in the delivery room:

"Why do you need an epidural? I didn't need a shot. They didn't give us a shot back then." She went on,

"I took the pain. *We* took the pain. I didn't need it. Y'all are weak. You can't take pain. You need to take the pain."

She really said that during my labor pains! In the middle of contractions! Twelve hours of labor. Just 30 minutes prior to her rant, I was almost paralyzed after jerking when the nurse tried to inject the epidural. The nurse fussed at me. I didn't have the energy to go into sister girl mode. I think my husband was holding me on one side of the bed then dragging me to the other side after the shot. The pain wrenched from my thighs to my pelvis to my back, my neck and head. The last two aches were compliments of my mother.

"You're weak," sitting with her arms folded and legs crossed under. She didn't even get up to help! Just ridiculed while I was bent over in excruciating pain. That did it! That was when I became Michael Jackson in that 1950s letterman jacket and flooded jeans getup, convulsing and transformed into that hideous creature in the *Thriller* video.

"*Run now!*"

Or at least that's how I pictured it.

I probably just rolled my eyes and told my mother to "*Shut up!*" in my head (lol emoji).

To add insult to injury, my mother sat within the perfect view to witness her 2nd granddaughter's birth and made faces that read 'yuck' and 'eww' the whole time! With her arms folded and legs crossed under, she jerked back every time a new disgusting image of her grandbaby was revealed from my vagina.

My poor husband saw everything while he held my right leg in place. He did all but endure the pain and have the baby for me. I'm surprised he could tolerate so much, let alone would dare to revisit *Time Square* after witnessing *Godzilla* destroy it (grinning squinting face emoji). He informed me later that he should have remained *Upstate* (smiling face with sweat emoji).

Nailah is a talented tot. She started reading at the age of 4; age 3 according to her. I could swear she came out of the womb talking. She has always been clingy and opinionated. She's smart like me, but smarter than me as my oldest brother, Charles Jr., informed me matter-of-factly. She's competitive and high maintenance. My husband and I had to admit that we did not appreciate our low maintenance son until we had our high maintenance daughter. If you give her the moon and the stars, she'll ask, "Where's the sun?"

Nailah is a true thespian. She studies people—their behavior. She can imitate, re-create and exaggerate. When she was 3, I was watching *Dora the Explorer* with her when she chimed that she wanted to "do that."

"What do you mean?" I asked her.

"I want to do what they are doing on tv with Dora."

"You mean the voices?"

"Yeah," she replied sucking her thumb in between responses.

"That's called a 'voice over'," I informed her.

"Yeah. I wanna do that," she said with confidence.

Turns out she wanted to do it all. She wrote her first script at age 7. She included multiple characters that her brother and cousins portrayed. She played the narrator. It was a project her Uncle Macon, challenged her to. I am embarrassed to admit I didn't think she would accomplish the task.

We were on a family vacation in South Carolina. Our family domestic trips were always planned by Charles Jr. We dreaded the roadway journeys but my brother never disappointed with the destinations. We always had a good time. This particular year there was my household of 4, my parents, my 4 sibs, 4 grandkids and the youngest one, my daughter, in tears for reasons unknown to me to this day. The trips always began chaotic then simmered by day 2. My Mini-me was accusing her big brother and cousin of doing something when my older brother, Macon, reminded her that she had a task that she was supposed to fulfill. I interjected,

"She didn't do it."

"I did do it!" She snapped.

I felt horrible, particularly because I thought I knew her every move. I never saw her jot down a thing that had anything to do with that project. I didn't want her uncle to be disappointed.

"Oh, I'm sorry Nini," I told her with motherly sincerity.

"Alright, let's hear it then." her Uncle Macon said in anticipation.

Nailah then went in her luggage and pulled out this multi-paged scripted play with a comical introduction along with assigned characters for her brother and cousins. A copy of the script for each actor and descriptions of their personas were attached. She perked up, red eyes now glowing, tears withdrawn. She stood erect and drew her audience in with her intro. The snotty nosed irritated little sister immediately warped into a writer, director, producer, and actress on demand. The script was 15 minutes long. It was so creative and beyond her years. The kid was 7! I never underestimated my "Mini-me" again. She's got it and I'm going to do all I can to help her prosper in it.

I learned from that and my own childhood experiences that the one thing your talented tot expresses a passion for should be at least the one thing you nurture to maturity. They will get distracted. It is within their nature to want to do other normal kid things which is fine. But prioritize nurturing the talent.

******

I was a bookworm. Nothing special there. There was something special about reading at a 5th grade level in the 1st grade. I fell in love with words and poetry in the 2nd grade. Robert Louis Stephenson was my favorite writer. Do you know another 7-year-old Black girl in love with a 19th century poet/fictional writer? I was obsessed with words and oratory. I wrote poems and short stories like they were assignments. I read encyclopedias for fun (and drew pictures in a few). I loved documentaries, fiction, and non-fiction. I read the book *Tom Sawyer* when I was 11 after my dad bought it for me. I read *Treasure Island* in the 4th grade. Again, do you know another? I wrote and read all the time. I read all the time until the 6th grade when my mom decided that I read too much and she stopped buying me books. Imagine that. She said I read too much. Consequently, unnurtured dreams of writing surrendered to common 6th grade girl dreams of becoming a pediatrician. Or maybe I would try something in math instead. That was my 2nd alternative career choice.

My oldest sister, Tracy, brought her accounting assignments home from college during her sophomore year and she let me double check her work using our dad's business calculator. Maybe accounting is my thing. By 7th grade I had no idea as to what I wanted to be. In high school I wanted to find a cure for cancer and by the end of 11th grade results from an aptitude test declared that I was going to be a pharmacist. So, my career aspirations shifted accordingly.

******

My mom informed me years later while I was in college that she was throwing all of my old stuff away because it was junking up her house (aka my old bedroom). She had a penchant for discarding "junk" she found. She said if I wanted all my awards and trophies that I needed to get them. I told her I did and not to toss anything else before I returned. It didn't dawn on me to tell her not to toss out my poems and stories. I was a mediocre artist so I didn't care so much about my drawings. But spare my writings please. Too late.

Dear parents,

Your children may show you very early on what they are born to be. It is the bulb that you are responsible for planting and watering. It is a talent that comes naturally and requires development. It may appear as an obsession but it's more appropriately designated as a passion. Pay attention to it. Encourage it. Nurture it.

I imagine there are many people who have talents or gifts that go unnurtured. Some of whom are probably my pharmacy peers. Especially if no one, including their parents, had an understanding and sometimes the resources, to nurture and navigate it. The consequence of unnurtured talent can lead to an unfulfilled life if you don't adapt and pivot to do something else that makes your life meaningful. Like some of my pharmacy peers had the courage to do in the middle of their careers. I imagine I'd be much better and further along with my writing skills had I chosen an appropriate major. But who's to say that the path I chose didn't lead me to right to where I'm supposed to be and when I was supposed to be there? Just maybe pharmacy was the rocky road I needed to travel to gain the resources, to have a story to tell, to get to purpose and fulfillment.

My mother knew the value of education and ownership. However, her purview was apropos to her past. *This was useful. That wasn't.* Her predilections were to rid her life of things not useful. It was her nature. Unclutter the clutter. She didn't know what to do with a reader/writer. Other than buying more books and encouraging me to read, neither did my dad to an extent. But I never counted it against them because they loved me and my older siblings so much and nurtured many other aspects of our lives.

I remember my mother would take me with her from time to time to visit the elders and the "sick and shut-ins" from our church. She would spend time with them like a friend. She was always active in our church; including serving as a clerk for over 30 years. I watched her pray, teach Sunday school, donate, give food and other necessities away to people in need. Today, I do the same; mimicking her. I didn't realize my mother was preparing me for ministry all those years while growing up.

Also, growing up, I wanted to join different clubs (not always for free) or gymnastics, go on school trips, play basketball, my dad recording those basketball games, or driving me to summer internship locations that were never local. My parents would always oblige. They never said no. Even when they had no clue as to what I was up to. Saying "yes" gave me the wings to succeed.

So, I'm not complaining here. Just dissecting a misread formula. I never fault my parents for what they didn't know or didn't have to give, remembering they gave us the greatest gift they could by giving us life, their support, and a happy home. Not to mention they shoved out a ton of money for my college education at a private university (hug and kiss emoji). It's better to show appreciation for everything they did do. My parents are two wonderful people. They made so many sacrifices and gave every good thing they had. I love them so much and I thank them both.

19

A Bitter-Sweet Pill to Swallow

During my second year of pharmacy school one of my professors, a physician, rearranged our class seating. Supposedly it was her response to some talkative and disrespectful students who undermined her during class. She was courteous enough to teach Pathophysiology to a group of uninterested pharmacy students who would have rather just skipped that phase of the curriculum. I liked her. She was no more than 5 ft. tall but by no means a pushover. She proved so the day she unsegregated the class. Subsequently, I ended up sitting to the right of an Indian American classmate. I'll call him "Mohinder." I previously knew him by name only. He was a loquacious, good-looking guy who was uninhibited and undisciplined by all accounts. His father was a clinician at one of the local hospitals. He noticeably looked nothing like his father.

Unfortunately, by proximity, I discovered Mohinder's indoctrinated side. I didn't so much think that he thought he was superior as I realized he'd been influenced by the wrong people. Or perhaps he was influenced by the father he didn't resemble. It's just that his attitude was very familiar to me. He'd make discriminatory comments. Knowing that he was a student at a historically Black college, I presumed he wouldn't dare say a negative word about Black people. At least not in front of a Black person. But I was shocked that he assumed that I'd be ok with hearing pejoratives about people who weren't Black. During a conversation Mohinder called Tulane, a prestigious university that was about 2 miles down the road, '*Jewlane*.' I was stunned. To hear that from a minority of minorities caught me off guard.

 "Why are you calling it that?," is how I responded. What I should have said was,

"*Don't* call it that," giving no room for my beliefs to be misconstrued.

I especially found it interesting that he could only know the demographic at that campus if he frequently visited that campus. Which would also imply that he found that campus to be welcoming and resourceful for study even though he wasn't paying a dime for it. And if that's the resource he used because Xavier's pharmacy library, for instance, didn't stay open long enough (it didn't) and didn't have enough study rooms (it did not), then what did he really think about his future alma mater and its demographic? What kind of person would say something like that? Probably the same kind that did not hold himself accountable for his own actions.

Mohinder complained toward the end of our academic career that he didn't feel like he learned anything. '*You probably didn't,*' I thought to myself. If he listened and studied half as much as he ran his mouth, he'd be a member of Rho Chi. But like me he wasn't. He was in the bottom half of the class, also like me. Unlike me, he was content with blaming all but himself for his lack of knowledge. *The only common denominator in every class every year is you. The problem is you!*

As for myself, what I didn't know, I didn't know. If I didn't read or study enough, then I can't expect the best grade. If I didn't retain what I read that was just mind over matter. But in reverse. I did not persevere and keep studying. I shut it down. When my brain says "enough," that's enough. Self-preservation takes over and that's ok. I didn't need to be an 'A' student. I needed to graduate. I needed to know how to navigate my chosen profession. I needed to know how to think and how to serve others exceptionally in a fast-paced environment. Connect with the right people. Connect with the customer/patient. Shadow successful pharmacists even if I couldn't stand them personally, so that I'd swim and not sink in an environment that I loved but didn't necessarily love me back. I needed an exit strategy for when I'd had enough of retail pharmacy. That required a financial cushion and putting faith into action. Even if I messed up (and I did), it's ok to try again or pivot and explore something else. Walk by faith, not by sight (2 Cor 5:7). My faith walk is unique to me. I can do all things, create, recreate, adapt, or move on. My success doesn't need to look like anyone else's.

What I need is to be satisfied with the work I've done as a supportive wife, mom, minister and pharmacist. What I need to be sure of is whether my presence in those roles has made a difference. Most importantly, am I serving my purpose? For me, purpose is centered in ministry. That calling penetrates into my professional and personal life. As for my personal life, I didn't do too bad.

My husband is an EHS manager with an Italian company. They're cool people. They value him in ways he hadn't experience with previous employers. So do the employees. I used to preach to Ron about knowing his worth and making a move. I also coached him on how to negotiate, to ask for more money and that it was ok to move on if he felt devalued. I did it myself—ask for raises when I believed I wasn't being compensated fairly. It resulted in 3 raises in one year (cheezy face emoji). I told Ron It was ok to be afraid to leave especially after investing so much time and building relationships. But don't allow those relationships to supersede your potential and what you deserve. Move on. Build new relationships. He did. He's finally content. No more 2 and ½ year itch. After 22 years of marriage, we've finally set up roots. We did it together (high 5 emoji).

Our kids are legally adults now. Our son, Malcolm, will be graduating from college soon. He's worked as a student IT assistant at Georgia Tech since his sophomore year in college. That position at Georgia Tech forged a pathway through which he can transition into a post-grad full-time position. It's a great starting point right out of college.

I enrolled Malcolm in IT summer camps when he was in grade school like those at UGA, Emagination located at GA Tech's campus at the time, and ID Tech at Emory University that would benefit him towards his future career. It makes me so thrilled that all those investments were not lost on him. Turns out individuals with his diagnosis often successfully choose Computer Science and IT as majors. His father and I are so proud of him (hug and kiss emoji).

As for my Mini-me, Nailah, she obtained a full scholarship to an in-state university (praise hands emoji!). This high maintenance child who I spent a fortune on in summer film camps, acting and dance classes, driving her all over the place, once in the middle of the night to make it to set on time as a background actress. If that wasn't enough, she's spending a semester on a ship traveling to multiple cities on three continents. She fell in love with theater and production. She never wavered since she was 3 years old on her career choice. I have to admit, she's working confidently in her field of study without my help these days. Still, I inserted my opinion that the real power is behind the camera. She decided to major in Film and Media with a minor in Entertainment Media Management. With a ton of experience by the time she completes her fourth year, I have no doubt, as her name insists, she will succeed.

******

When I look back at the episodes from college to mid-life and my career, has it all been worth it? Even as things did not go as originally planned, has my presence mattered? Do I make a difference? To sum things up, I live to serve. I go where I am useful. I believe I make a difference with leading small groups. It matters that I call or text group members and love ones just to check in to see how they are doing. I make a difference when I genuinely listen to them. I pray with them and for them. I will always be active in church. I will always serve in some capacity in or outside of church. Ministry even follows me to work.

When I consider my life so far as a pharmacist, what I know is that when others enjoy working around me, not all do, but when they ask questions that eventually lead to biblical conversations, my biblical knowledge matters. Or when technicians' attitudes become welcoming after challenging me due to lack of trust, I make a difference. I offer peace and a listening ear. I know I make a difference when they share family pictures and personal stories. Or if I'm asked,

"Where have you been?"

"When are you coming back?"

Or if I'm told not to leave. I'm a floater. I'm definitely leaving (smile emoji). I know I make a difference when a person's day is made better after visiting the pharmacy, sometimes working in towns where some people are shown empathy while others are shown apathy. When I save customers money by calling the doctor's office for a cheaper medicine or using coupons or vouchers—that matters. Think of the difference it makes to just care more. Even when it's not convenient. When I ease a customer's anxiety about a drug or their condition, it matters. I know I have an impact after counseling an HIV patient for nearly 30 minutes convincing them that taking their medicine and adjusting to this new norm is not the end of the world. But that choosing to be adherent is choosing to live. The extra time I take to double check a dose for a new prescription is not in vain. I know that after driving well over an hour to get to a pharmacy location and being 5 minutes late only to be greeted with smiles because it's me, that I matter. So, yes. My presence *has* made a difference.

No promotions. I either turned it down or didn't stick around long enough to pursue. No accolades. No parties unless you count those going away cake-n-punch gatherings. I'm not even a church leader unless you count small group. I honestly saw my life being way more exciting than this when I was a teenager. I thought I'd be living out of a suitcase. Yet, I am right where I'm supposed to be, serving my purpose. Making a difference. I hope you are too. It's like a prescription drug if it was made human. I am someone, made by *Someone*, whose mechanism of action has an effect on a countless number of lives. We all have an MOA by *divine design* intended to help and not hurt.

******

I admit to leaning heavily on a greater than average GPA from my first couple of years in pre-pharm and did as much as possible to distract from an all-consuming curriculum that could and for a few students did cause a nervous breakdown. One of my distractions was the Homework Clinic where I volunteered tutoring 3rd through 5th grade students after school. I loved it. It was a great outlet and benefited those kids academically and socially. The exceptions were those afternoons where no matter what you offered those babies, they were just mentally exhausted and "checked out" by the time they got to me and the other tutors. They'd engage in anything accept homework and productivity. Occasionally, we got them on track by withholding snacks until they completed homework. Otherwise, on those days, talking about private family biz or even farting then bursting into laughter was more amusing to them than absorbing any more structured curriculum. In a weird way, I totally understood. For sanity's sake we all need those freeing moments to decompress (lol emoji).

As for the rest of my comrades during that time in pharmacy school, I heard that same statement Mohinder deferred to multiple times, '*I didn't learn anything.*' I think it was conjured from fear rather than revelation. We had so much information compressed into our brains over a truncated amount of time. Then instructors had the nerve to test us as if we could regurgitate it all in a couple of hours during exams. If your short-term memory was good then you were good. But if your nature was to rely on your long-term knowledge, well you might be screwed for those exams. Realistically, we all actually learned more than we thought, nerves aside.

The licensing exams we all had to pass to become registered pharmacists ranged from easy peasy to wtf?! The questions believe it or not, adjust in real-time according to your answers. If the algorithm thinks you know enough of one topic, it moves on. If you get enough answers wrong, you get more questions on the same topic. If you were unlucky, and the exam shifts to a topic you know nothing about... may the force be with you (rotfl!). Nonetheless, most graduates pass the licensing exam the first time. For the remaining test dummies, well, second time's the charm (grinning face emoji).

A year or so after we were licensed, those of us living in Georgia, heard from a local news report that Flipp Warrant, our NAPLEX prep instructor, was arrested for helping students obtain old questions from licensing exams. They were charged with copyright infringement. Not once did it occur to me, or anyone else as far as I knew, that a crime was being committed with those prep courses. They were K-type questions, or basically all or nothing questions. They could easily trip you up. I thought they were preparing our brains to think the way instructors think—to see the bigger picture. But apparently not. Apparently, we were just cheating. Again, if you memorize and test well, you're good; if not, oh well. It's the pump and dump. Memorize enough to pass the test. Dump that info afterwards because you'll never see it again. Nonetheless, people like myself and Mohinder, the smart dummies with long-term knowledge made out just fine in our careers.

Most of us chose community pharmacy right out of school as it fit our multitasking, ADHD personalities. Even today, twenty plus years later, some are still bearing those insane shifts and the saga of face-to-face, pill popping, community care. One classmate jokingly told me he was 'working like a Hebrew slave.' Probably because he's living like a Pharoah (lol emoji). I heard Mohinder and a couple of other classmates became directors at hospitals. Other careers ranged from clinicians to community pharmacists and managers, to independent pharmacy owners and non-related entrepreneurs. I became a career floater pharmacist who's experienced enough for two lifetimes and three books. It has also been a position that has given me freedom to choose, to maintain my sanity, to prioritize and actually enjoy this life. Among other things, I swing trade, I'm a property manager and now author. Yes, I'm all over the place and it suits me. Thank God there's a thousand ways to make money. I believe my parents give me the side-eye as if they waisted *their* money on my education. They didn't. They're reminded on birthdays, holidays and whenever we take family trips with *my* money.

Despite my brain being fried from retail and subsequently bowing out of the hell hole hamster wheel, I *did* learn a lot from my work experiences. I have no regrets. I remember some need-to-know things from pharmacy school, also. I remember why magnesium may be given to a patient who has low potassium, and why high doses of lidocaine are contraindicated for an epileptic, that Lexapro is better taken in the evening to avoid the jittery side effects, and why Omeprazole and Plavix in the elderly should be avoided, other drug-drug, drug-therapy interactions, etc., etc. It just happens to be that a lot of what I learned in pharmacy school went unused in community pharmacy. We're taught to be clinicians not *chicos de la esquina.*

******

What pharmacy schools should seriously consider embedding in the curriculum is a psyche course with real world customer service scenarios. Not like those HR generated on-the-job training modules with fake customers and fake interactions. There are instances where we cannot satisfy everyone. There are times when those encounters end with insults from the customer or yelling. What do we say? What do we do?

We multitask. We get overwhelmed. Then we deal with that supervisor who constantly complains and cannot spell the word "compliment." We are human beings under those white coats. They should consider that much effort is required of us as health care providers with little trained psychological support. How we are treated by higher ups matter. How we treat the people we serve matters. How we are treated by the people we serve matters. Outcomes from our services matter. Integrity matters. How we feel at the end of a shift or by the end of our careers matter. It has to be worth it.

Students in pharmacy school should receive multiple visits from seasoned community pharmacists giving them the real deal. I also suggest physical education or self-defense classes as well. I do. Preferably karate. All designed to prep the body and mind for the unimaginable storms to come. Pharmacists must learn to not react in addition to being proactive. We also have to leverage our personal and professional lives. Know what we're signing up for. The revolving door of the business is a reality many do not foreshadow. Pharmacy grads are NOT trained for the psychological impact of community pharmacy. That has to change.

This pharmacy career has been anything but linear. It's actually been as kinky as my 4c hair. I've worked and witnessed enough to lose every strand. It's a tough gig. But our services make a difference. Like my fellow comrades and especially my fellow pharmacy sisters, I hang in there. By that I mean we cling to a coping mechanism, whatever that may be, until we verify our very last prescription. Until that day comes, with humility and appreciation, I'll serve *sparingly* with my fifth and final pharmaceutical company. Where's that you might ask? "The Moon." I work on "The Moon." There's still never a dull day.

ABOUT THE AUTHOR

Angie LaShaye (pen name) is a graduate of Xavier University of Louisiana College of Pharmacy. She is licensed in the state of Georgia and practices in behavioral health services. Angie obtained a Master of Arts in Ministry degree in 2020 from Luther Rice College and Seminary, serving previously as an associate minister, young adult ministry leader, current small group leader, and volunteer. Angie has been married for over twenty years and has 2 children. Her passions include writing, ministry, traveling, human rights advocacy, and helping those in need.